New Brighton Area High School
New Brighton, Pennsylvania

Roads That Seldom Curve

*Before Al Allen became
the renowned artist, teacher,
and storyteller he is today,
there were his years growing up
along the Mississippi.
These are his remembrances,
vividly embracing and
occasionally challenging
our own memories of times
we think of as simpler.*

Roads That Seldom Curve

Al Allen

with Jeanie Flake Frauenthal

August House Publishers, Inc.
LITTLE ROCK

Published by August House, Inc.,
P.O. Box 3223, Little Rock, Arkansas, 72203,
501/372-5450.

Printed in the United States of America
10 9 8 7 6 5 4 3 2 1

LIBRARY OF CONGRESS
CATALOGING-IN-PUBLICATION DATA

Allen, Al, 1925-
Roads that seldom curve : growing up along the Mississippi /
Al Allen with Jeanie Flake Frauenthal.
p. .cm
ISBN 0-87483-168-7 (hardback : acid-free) : $19.95 —
ISBN 0-87483-167-9 (pbk. : acid-free) : $9.95
1. Missouri—Social life and customs. 2. Allen, Al, 1925- —Childhood and
youth. 3. Pemiscot County (Mo.)—Biography. 4. Allen family.
I. Frauenthal, Jeanie Flake. II. Title.
F466.A42   1991
977.8'99604'092—dc20
[B]   90-26880

First Edition 1991

Executive: Ted Parkhurst
Project editor: Judith Faust
Cover design: Communication Graphics
Typography: Lettergraphics, Little Rock

Cover painting: "Blue Sanctum," 1982, 48" x 60", acrylic,
by Al Allen.

This book is printed on archival-quality paper which meets
the guidelines for performance and durability of the
Committee on Production Guidelines for Book Longevity
of the Council on Library Resources.

AUGUST HOUSE, INC. PUBLISHERS LITTLE ROCK

To Eric,
my son and my joy

Contents

The highest knowledge is to know that we are surrounded by mystery.

ALBERT SCHWEITZER

Prologue

Crossroads

When summer finally came and school let out, my father carried me up the river to the Bootheel to stay a while with Uncle Will. Up there the land was rich with bottom sand and so flat that you could see a water tower eight miles away glittering in the evening sun or see a thunder cloud in time to reach the storm house long before the wind and rain would come. The roads all led north and south and east and west and seldom curved at all, and the dust was always ankle-deep like summer snow. The warm summer air carried sounds and smells about with an easy pace that made for joy and peace.

My uncle's farmhouse was the only one around for miles except for the Craigs', across the road and down a piece. They had a daughter named Martha Sue, who was thirteen. Her eyes and hair were rich dark brown, and when I saw her again after the long winter months, she would hug me hard and kiss me on the cheek. It was with her that I would climb the poplar tree until the narrow limbs gave and swayed, and then she would climb on higher still and laugh in love as I clung below. She taught me how to run, to worm a hook, to shuck the corn, to call pigs and crow, to sing, to laugh and never to cry.

Sometimes we would eat cold biscuits crammed with jam and gather berries off the levee bank. Sometimes we would roam across the deep alfalfa to a lone pear tree where we would eat and talk of tall city buildings, of street cars and Ferris wheels, and on the day they cut the hay, we would chase the baby rabbits for a while. It was Martha Sue who knew the time by the shadows on the ground or by the whistle of a train that blew across the county line.

In her father's barn were many cribs of feed and corn, and we would sometimes lie in the loft upon the cotton seed and talk of God and love, and there she showed me once all her body that had not felt the sun and showed me, too, a chicken snake curled upon a rafter. With her, I watched the field hands slowly come and go in song, and in the evening we would laugh at the mules so free from harness as they played and wallowed in the dirt. She made it clear to me how calves were born, and from time to time we watched the sow and boar.

Late one day, she called me back behind her smokehouse door and softly spoke and looked about with care. "I've got a secret," she whispered low, "and you must swear to God that you will not tell a soul on earth what you will see and hear today." I gave my solemn oath, and then she grabbed my hand and down the road we ran until we grew tired, and then we walked a while.

"You see this sty here on my eye?" she asked. I answered with a nod. "I'm going to cast it off on someone else with secret words that I have learned." Her voice was sure and sly.

We ran some more. At last, far down the road, we reached another road that crossed our way, and now the sun was low. The sand was cooling on our feet. She looked all ways, but nothing was in sight.

"Stand a little down the road and wait," she said quietly, "for once I say the magic words, this crossroad is condemned."

I stood and watched as she scratched a circle in the sand just where the roads did cross, and then she stood inside it, looked straight up into the sky, and recited softly:

> *Hokum, spokum, rigomoo rye,*
> *Man must live and man must die,*
> *Hokum, spokum, sty on eye*
> *Be on the next one passes by.*

She said it a second time, and then a third, and then she dashed by me running as fast as she could toward home. I ran after her as the day grew grey, and finally she began to walk and I caught up. We walked backwards for a piece looking far back into the darkness to the crossroad, but there was no one there.

"Will it really work, Martha Sue?" I asked, still breathing a little hard.

"Sure it will," she said. "The next person who goes by that crossroad will get my sty and I will lose it. Just you wait and see." We walked along in silence, kicking at the sand, and when we got closer home we heard her father call, so we ran on the rest of the way.

That night, I lay listening to the night birds calling out in the darkness and wondered what held the stars up in the sky. I thought of Martha Sue and all her magic and wondered who would get her sty, and then I dreamed a while.

It was still dark the next morning when I slipped into my overalls and quietly crept outside and slowly ran back down the road. The light raced across the sky with a distant rooster's crow, and a gentle breeze made the sunflowers move and look at me. When I got real near to the very spot where Martha Sue had stood, I jumped a ditch and sat behind some weeds. The sun was up and warm. Bugs began to hop and the dew disappeared.

My heart beat faster when at last I heard a sound, a singing voice, far down the eastbound road. It was for sure someone coming to the spot where Martha Sue had cast her magic words. I lay down low and breathed with care. Louder still a man sang, and then at last he crossed the very place. He took two steps beyond and stopped and sang no more. He turned quickly and looked straight back down the road from which he came, and then he turned to right and left with hard and searching eyes, but he only saw a sparrow fanning in the sand. He rubbed his eye, turned slowly, began to sing again, and continued on his way.

When I could hear his voice no more, I leaped across the ditch and ran all the way to the Craigs' woods lot. I crossed a barbed-wire fence and raced across their open yard. There sitting on the back porch was Martha Sue, chopping cabbage up for kraut with her mother churning nearby. I saw her sparkling eyes, and both were clear as crystal, and there was no sty. She smiled at me and held her head so proud. Her mother hummed a little tune. I just sat and watched her as I ate a cabbage core. I sure did love that Martha Sue.

1

The Hanging Man

ONE DAY WHEN I was about five years old, I was playing in our front yard in Steele, Missouri, when my daddy drove up and told me to get in the car. It was a brand new, dark green Chevy coupe with a rumble seat. "I'm taking you for a ride," he said. My mother came out on the front porch, and Daddy told her we would be back in a little while.

I stood in the front seat and held on to the back of it while he drove north on Highway 61. We went about twelve miles and turned left after crossing the Frisco Railroad. Then we went a short piece down a dirt road to a little town called Braggadocio. Daddy pulled off the road and killed the engine. There, just across the road, was a man hanging by his neck from a tree. Three or four small groups of people were looking at him from a distance. The man looked dirty and muddy—the color of a towsack. We just sat there in the car for what seemed to be a very long time without saying anything. Daddy could be very quiet. I waited. Finally, I asked, "What happened?"

"The man did wrong," Daddy said.

We sat there another five minutes. Daddy started the car and we rode back home in silence.

A little more than half a century later when I was teaching in Little Rock, I got a letter from Beulah Allen, who lived back home, out from Caruthersville. It began, "You probably don't remember me. I'm one of your lost cousins, the daughter of your Uncle John." She said she had last visited with me when I was about fourteen, but she had seen me from a distance since I'd been grown, when I had been back to Missouri for funerals. She had read a story about my paintings in the Memphis *Commercial Appeal,* she said, and often wondered about me and my family. She invited me to come up to the Bootheel, and said she'd round up all my cousins for a visit. She ended the letter by saying, "Your daddy was always my favorite uncle."

Early in the summer of 1983, I wrote her to say I'd be in that area taking photographs for my work and I'd be very happy to come visit.

I arrived at Beulah's on a Sunday morning about eleven o'clock. She greeted me at the door and hugged me, and I was shocked to see how old she was, though I knew she was ten years older than I. She took me in the house and introduced me to two families who had already arrived. Soon cars and trucks were driving up, bringing the families of the sons and daughters of my father's eleven older brothers and sisters. Many of them seemed strange to me, and they all seemed older than they ought to have been. These people I had always thought of as "my young cousins" were in their sixties, seventies, and maybe eighties.

Soon the women congregated in the kitchen to prepare the meal, and I sat in the living room with nine old men. I had been introduced to everyone, but was utterly confused about who was whose child and who was married to whom. I couldn't connect any names with faces except for Beulah's. While we waited for dinner, the men carried on several loud, simultaneous conversations about their crops, businesses, and jobs. It didn't seem right for me to offer stories about my job as a university art professor or about my last exhibition. I felt awkward and out of place as they talked about cotton and tractors, but I got really uncomfortable when the talk turned to people they knew who had died and to the agonizing natures of the deaths. So I sat, feeling neglected and a little sorry for myself, until I realized these were the sons of all my wonderful uncles, who were never as warm and hugging as my aunts.

Presently a female cousin came out of the kitchen to tell us dinner was ready, and we went back where there were three long tables set up. Beulah asked me to say grace, an honor extended to one returned to the fold. I recalled a standard Mississippi dinner blessing learned from my wife's family, and worded it carefully so as not to offend them, I thought. But at the end, I said something about "increasing our tolerance for one another"—it slipped out—and tucked in one of my pet phrases about "our search for ultimate truth." When I finished, I noticed that they were looking at me a bit strangely. But we had a lavish meal of three kinds of meat, gravy, three kinds of potatoes, at least five different dishes of fresh vegetables, good yeast rolls, and every female cousin's masterpiece dessert. They were all great cooks, just like my aunts; the Allen ritual of eating hadn't changed at all.

After dinner, the men gathered again in the living room, and I began to wonder if I might be responsible for the silence, if maybe they didn't know what to talk about because I was there.

Finally, one cousin began to speak about my father. "Old Alvin was really something," he said. Soon they were all talking about going to the county fair back in the thirties and watching my father drive a car at full speed around a horse track, dragging a man by a rope behind the car. The man was some kind of roving professional drag person who showed up at big county fairs and called for the fastest driver in the crowd to tie one end of a rope to a car bumper and the other end to his ankles. He wore only a pair of Tuff Nutt overalls when Daddy pulled him four times around the track. The official fair board selected Daddy for the job, making it quite an honor.

"Yeah," another cousin said, "Old Alvin could get anywhere in a car. I remember he once took a doctor out to Number Eight when a woman out there was deathly ill. The doctor couldn't get through the gumbo mud. The woman's family called Alvin, and he got the doctor to her. It was in the county paper how he saved her life."

Then another cousin opened the subject of Uncle Louis, who drank more than all the other uncles and was most feared by his neighbors. He was eternally threatening to cut off little children's ears. "Many's the time I've seen him down at Cotton-wood Point buying groceries when he'd grab some young boy, pull out his knife, and say, 'I'm gonna cut off your ears,'" the cousin said. Another added that the law went out to Uncle Louis's house several times to tell him to quit scaring people to death. They talked on about that for ten more minutes.

I wanted to join in, and finally made myself do it. "Yes, I was with my daddy when the law called from Caruthersville and told him to come get Uncle Louis or they were going to put him in jail," I said. "So we went and got Uncle Louis and carried him to his home right off the levee at Cottonwood Point. When we were still a half a mile away, he saw a couple of old cars and a mule and wagon out in front of his house and started cursing and shouting, 'She's got those church women in my house again!' I guess Aunt Etter had thought he'd be gone all day and had invited the church circle over. When we drove up, he got out yelling and started picking up brickbats and throwing them at the house. Aunt Etter and the rest of the women came running out the side door and into the field, and he threw brickbats at *them*. Daddy tried to calm him down, but he was a maniac. When Uncle Louis was sure they were all out of the house, he stomped in and went to sleep. The women crept back to their vehicles and left, and Aunt Etter finally went back in the house."

"Yeah, he was a cutter, all right," someone concluded.

"You know, we didn't have a grandmother because she died giving birth to Old Alvin," another one started. I knew this story well. "Aunt Annie had just lost a baby a few days before, so when our grandmother died, they just gathered Alvin up and took him down to Aunt Annie, and she raised her little brother like her own baby."

"That's right," another one said. "And Grandfather died in three weeks. Died of grief."

"And, you know, Old Alvin didn't find out that Annie was his sister till he was about thirteen—found it out at school one day and then disappeared for several weeks, but he finally came back."

After a pause, someone said to me, "Alvin Junior, you sure had a pretty mother. I guess Carrie was the most sought-after girl in the county before she married your daddy." Then they all recounted how Ed Harkreader had become my father's lifelong enemy after Daddy had saved his money for months to buy Carrie's cake at a social when he first started courting her, only to be outbid by Harkreader. "Of course, Old Alvin finally made good in the car business. Why, he sold over five hundred cars back in thirty-six. Paper had a picture of him in front of his business."

"Sure did. He was a good provider. I never did understand why Carrie thought she had to move off to Memphis to get a job when the Depression hit."

"Yeah, it's hard to figger."

I said nothing; I hadn't figured it out either. When I was six and Mother told me she and I—without Daddy—were moving to Memphis, I just accepted it as something my mother had decided to do. She told me I could go to better schools in Memphis.

By that time, the women had finished the dishes and wandered into a slight lull in tale-telling. I summoned up my courage and said, "There's something I want to ask since everyone's here. I remember Daddy carrying me up to Braggadocio when I was about five and showing me a man hanging from a tree. What was that all about?"

Suddenly, there was dead silence. The male cousins all looked at one another in disbelief. So I asked it again and added, "I talked to Uncle Willis just before he died about three years ago, and all he said was that the hanging had really happened." The awkward quiet went on, and I remembered that Uncle Willis had acted a little funny, too.

Finally, one of the men asked, "You mean to tell me that Old Alvin carried you over to see the Brewster man hanging?"

"Yeah," I said. "He told me to get in the car one day, and we drove over and just sat there and looked a long time."

There was silence again, abruptly broken when a cousin said, "Hell, I was twenty-two and my daddy wouldn't let me go see that hanging." Then he got up, turned to his wife, and said, "I think it's time we go."

Soon everyone was finding it was time to go. The last one who left turned to me and said, "Nobody here got to see that man hanging from the tree. I heard that they dragged that man all over the county for about a half a day before they hung him."

It seemed to me they all left in a huff, some without even saying goodby. But Beulah was unrattled and remained kind and gracious to me as I thanked her and got in my own car.

I left and drove down the narrow highway that ran straight west from Caruthersville. When I got to Highway 61, a sign said "Braggadocio, 3 miles." I crossed the Frisco Railroad and drove down into the little town. It was dusk, and the town seemed almost deserted; there were only about four houses that looked inhabited. I stopped where I thought the hanging tree had been, but the tree wasn't there. I heard a mother hollering for her boy to come home because it was getting dark. The boy didn't come. In a while, I saw the mother come out of a house and go down the gravel road. Soon she came from around an old gray building, pulling the boy by the back of his shirt. When she got to her front yard, she grabbed a switch and began whipping him. His crying echoed up and down the empty street. I guess the boy had done wrong.

2

Uncle Will

SUNDAY AFTERNOONS AT UNCLE Will and Aunt Annie's were usually uneventful periods of rest and digestion. Aunt Annie frowned on too much activity on the Lord's Day. But one July Sunday when I was five years old was different.

I was trying to stay awake, listening to the grownups talk in the living room, when we all heard a double shotgun blast. I looked out the window and saw a black man carrying a shotgun on his shoulder walking west at a good clip on the far ditch bank. Uncle Will, who had been sitting on the front porch, saw him too. He came in and told us he was going to go see what had happened. I tagged along with him as he walked quietly across the Cooter Ditch.

Uncle Will didn't make me hold his hand, so I ran in and out of the cotton rows, making grasshoppers jump and chasing an occasional butterfly. Suddenly, I almost stepped on a black man lying between the rows, shot right in the middle, almost in half. Blood was all over the green cotton.

I called Uncle Will, who was just a few rows over. He came through the high cotton, looked down at the dead man, and said nothing. He took me out of the field and told me to stand in the road and wait a while. He went back into the field, took off his jumper, and put it over the dead man's head. He came and took my hand, and we walked back to the house at exactly the same pace we had come. He didn't say anything, but I quit trembling after a few minutes because I knew I didn't have to be afraid with Uncle Will.

When we got to the house, Uncle Will had Aunt Annie call the sheriff, who drove out as soon as he could and listened to Uncle Will describe the man he had seen carrying a shotgun and walking west on the far ditch bank. "If you hurry, you'll probably find the man who did it trying to catch the four-twenty freight near the state line," he told the sheriff. In about an hour, the sheriff came back by. There was a black man handcuffed in the back seat of the car. He had caught him on the railroad track, going toward the state line.

It was getting dark when the sheriff left. I helped Uncle Will feed and water the stock. We ate supper by a coal oil lamp and sat on the porch a little while. I went to bed in the dark, dark night and didn't think it a bit unusual that Uncle Will had known exactly where that man with the shotgun could be found, because Uncle Will had always known things.

While folks in the county came to Aunt Annie for healing and interpretations of scripture, they came to Uncle Will because of his almost mystical knowledge of nature. He knew when and where to plant, when to harvest, when to kill hogs, and all things about animals and mule ailments. He would walk around the ditch banks as far as a half mile on both sides to determine where to plant peanuts—never in the same place twice—and people always came begging for his peanuts.

No one in that part of the county would start anything until Uncle Will said it was time to begin. And whenever I visited, not a day passed that someone didn't knock on the porch and say, "Brother Will, I need to talk to you." Uncle Will would get two straight chairs and carry them out under the shade tree in the front yard. He would offer one to the visitor and straddle the other, resting his chin on his folded arms across its back. He wouldn't say a word while his neighbor told of a problem with mules or whatever. Then he would look off toward the fields—he was not an eye-looker—and give a three- or four-word answer. They'd get up and Uncle Will would take the chairs back into the house.

Uncle Will was not a big man; he stood an average five-ten. But he had very broad shoulders and was considered stout for good reason. I have seen him pull two twelve-foot sacks and pick two rows of cotton at once. His great, strong hands gathered all the cotton from the right-hand stalk in one sweeping, upward movement, scooped it into his right-hand sack, and then continued their instinctive movement from the top of the stalk on the other row downward. The field hands he oversaw for John Barnes Thompson's farm tried to imitate him but couldn't. In his seventies, he could steadily chop cotton from sunup to sundown with all the young men. He was known to have picked more than six hundred pounds of cotton in a day on several occasions, and even when he was seventy-two, he picked five hundred pounds of cotton a day for five straight days.

This made all his relatives and all the politicians in Pemiscot County do their best to get him to enter the World Cotton-Picking Championship down at Blytheville, Arkansas, which was always won by people who picked only in the four hundreds. When they'd try to convince him, Uncle Will would simply say, "I think not," even though the prize was one thousand dollars cash money. He just kept plugging along in the fields, wearing long johns and two jumpers straight through summer. He believed in trapping sweat as a coolant and insulating against the heat.

Uncle Will had had to quit school in the fourth grade. He didn't know his letters, but he knew his figures and kept accurate records for sixty to seventy field hands. He also weighed cotton for everybody in the county. No one ever questioned his weighing; he had started building his reputation for honesty when he first came to the Bootheel, while the land was still being drained and cleared. He had come from North Carolina into Tennessee, loaded stock onto log barges near Gayoso Bend, and crossed the Mississippi where the current threw them onto a sand bar in Missouri near Caruthersville. He had used his knowledge and stamina to become more successful than most farmers in the Bootheel and could therefore be categorized financially as an upper poor person, able to afford a barber-shop shave and haircut every week. He never shaved in between trips, so for the good part of the week he wore a short gray bristle that seemed appropriate for his role as the county sage. About the only other things he spent money on regularly were coal oil, salt, tobacco, vinegar, and matches. No one in the family drank coffee, and he raised everything else they needed. He even made the whiskey he used for his nightly toddies, which Aunt Annie condemned even though he only drank a small one before bed and had never been drunk in his life.

One day in the early thirties, a truck drove up to the home place, and a man got out and started telling Uncle Will how great it was that an ice truck would run that coming summer, a first for the county. The man explained to him that he'd have to buy an ice box and then went on to describe how much better drinks taste with ice: iced tea, iced lemonade, and even iced sweet milk. He told Uncle Will he could buy an ice cream freezer and make his own ice cream right at home with only one block of ice. When the man finally wound down, Uncle Will just said, "I tried ice over in Blytheville a couple of summers ago, and we don't want it here." So the ice truck didn't run in that part of Pemiscot County.

Perhaps the most mysterious thing about Uncle Will was his instinctive knowledge of cyclone behavior. Everybody in the Bootheel knew that Uncle Will's hay barn would blow away once every ten years. The story went that back before the turn of the century, just after the land had been cleared, a bad cyclone came through and blew nothing away but that hay barn. Uncle Will built it back right on the same spot, and from then on, about every ten years that hay barn would go. I asked him once why they didn't rebuild it somewhere else. Uncle Will said, "Better the barn to go than the house." So they kept on rebuilding the sacrificial barn in its appointed place, which was about three hundred yards north of the house, near the hay field.

Just before dark one night, we were sitting on the porch after a hard day's work. I was fourteen years old, and it was the last full summer I would spend in the Bootheel. It became a very dark, clear, moonless night. The stock had all been secured, but the mules seemed a little restless and the night sounds of the birds and bugs were quieter than normal. Without saying a word,

Uncle Will got up and rounded the corner of the house to the back. I followed him back to the barnyard fence, where he stood for about ten minutes and looked directly into the northwest. I said nothing, having learned long ago not to talk to him at certain times. Then he turned and began to pick up large poles and prop them against the hen house. He propped one firmly against the smokehouse. I followed him through a gate out to the mule barn. He took big tree-poles and leaned them against all the barn doors. I asked if I could help, and he said I could pull some tree-poles around to the other side of the barn. We left the barnyard and went to the side of the house, where he opened the storm house door.

"Why are you doing all of this, Uncle Will?"

"It's going to storm and blow real hard before morning."

That was hard to believe because there wasn't a cloud in the sky and not a sign of a storm as far the eye could see. After he checked to make sure the cellar lamp had plenty of coal oil, we came back around to the front yard. Uncle Will stopped for a minute and looked back at the unsecured hay barn, but we didn't go there.

About three o'clock that morning, there was a distant rumble, and it wasn't long till the thunder and lightning were near. Aunt Annie, who was deathly afraid of cyclones, hollered at us to hurry to the storm house. We got there in plenty of time before the storm hit and sat quietly by lantern light in front of Aunt Annie's perfect rows of canned peaches, tomatoes, chow-chow, and green beans. Uncle Will, as always, sat on the steps that led down from the door. Even if we stayed all night, he would not move from the steps.

In several minutes we could tell by tremendous thunder, very hard rain, and an occasional thud on the tin roof of the storm house that the storm was right above us. When it was over, we scurried toward the house because it was still raining a little. I glanced across the field and saw the hay barn was standing. Several limbs were down in the yard, but there was no major damage.

At breakfast, I asked Uncle Will, "How'd you know that storm was coming?"

He didn't say anything for a bit. Then with a slight smile he said, "You learn," and got up to start another day's work.

A little over a year later, during the late fall, news came to us in Memphis that a cyclone had again blown the hay barn away. By the time I went for a short visit the next summer, it was back up and painted a fresh red.

While waiting for my draft notice in 1944, I went by the home place to tell everyone good-bye. I had never seen Uncle Will cry, but there were large, ominous tears rolling from his eyes on the day I left. He looked as if he knew something I didn't. I never saw him again; he died while I was overseas.

A few years after the war, I was driving from Memphis to St. Louis and decided to go by the home place even though Aunt Annie was living with her niece twenty miles north of Cooter. When I got there, I saw that the hay barn was gone again. Some field hands along the road told me a bad cyclone had blown it away the previous fall and that the new family on the home place did not plan to replace it. Foolish, I thought.

Two years later I drove by again on a summer day, and the old house was gone, too. I wasn't surprised. Several years after that, I returned to find a new house built on the old home place lot, and there wasn't a hay barn in sight. I knew those people needed to be told what to do to secure their house, but only someone like Uncle Will had the authority to do that. Evidently, no one in Pemiscot County had taken his place in advising people when, where, and how to do the basic things of life.

3

Going North

IN 1935, JUST AFTER my tenth Christmas, our family drove up from Memphis to visit my grandmother in the Bootheel. She and her family were of the upper poor people during the Depression and lived in a big gray house about a mile from the Mississippi River levee and about six miles from the river town of Cottonwood Point. The only other house for miles around was a little shotgun shack up the road a piece; both houses were built on a dirt road in the middle of a massive cotton farm.

It had not snowed that winter, but it had been a bitter cold season with many dark blue days, and the flat land and dead fields made things quite bleak. We arrived late in the day, and it was dark before supper was ready. As we all gathered in the large room that served for both cooking and eating, my grandmother told my youngest aunt, Virginia, "Go call the boys."

Virginia went to the front yard and hollered down the road, "Cecil!" I heard a reply in the darkness. "Supper's ready," she called.

In about five minutes, two thin, shabbily dressed boys came in the front door. I learned later that Cecil was ten years old and his brother a year younger. My grandmother greeted them warmly and said, "Eat your supper, boys." They went over to a small table set up on the other side of the room. Without saying anything to anyone, they sat down, dug in, and had eaten everything on their plates long before we finished. They got up and came by the big table. Cecil said shyly to grandmother, "Thank you, Mrs. Bradie, for the food." My grandmother, a stoic woman with some Indian blood, acknowledged their thanks, and they went out into the darkness.

As it was in those days, I had been trained not to ask the grown folks too many questions about anything, but later on that night as we sat around the fire, I got brave enough to ask my Aunt Virginia about the boys. All she would tell me was that they lived down the road in that little shotgun shack.

The next morning, Virginia called the boys for breakfast, and then again for dinner at twelve, and again that night for supper. After each meal, Cecil said, "Thank you, Mrs. Bradie, for the food," and they left. So it was for our four-day visit. I never saw the boys outside of their house—it was near freezing—except for one slightly warmer day when I saw them sitting very still on their porch and watching up the road.

On the day we were to leave, Aunt Virginia told me that back in early November, the boys' mother and father had gone over to the Greenway Gin and Store for some groceries and had never come home. A few days later, my grandmother went down to their house and found them sitting around a cold stove, very quiet and very hungry. She brought them up to the big house for some food, and she had fed them every day since. Pete, my grandpa, had carried them wood to burn in their small stove.

My mother never let me go down and play. Just before we left to return to Memphis, I saw the boys sitting on their porch again, looking up the road.

In the spring, we again visited my grandmother. Just after we got there, I listened carefully as Aunt Virginia told my mother what had happened to the boys since our last visit.

In early February, a man came by my grandmother's house and told her the boys' mother and father had left the Greenway Gin and Store that November day and gone north on Brasher Road. People on Highway 61 had seen the man and woman walking north toward Hayti, and some people out from Hayti had seen them going north toward Portageville. My grandmother had Aunt Virginia call the boys over, and the man told them the same details.

The next day, Aunt Virginia said, just before noon there was a knock on the front porch, and the boys were standing there. Cecil said to my grandmother, "We're going to find Mama and Papa." My grandmother gave them a small sack of food and a dollar.

The boys went past the Greenway Gin and Store and went north on the Brasher road to Highway 61. It was reported at Hayti that the boys were seen about dark going north toward Portageville. The next day some people at Portageville said they saw two small boys on the outskirts of town, going north.

4

John Barnes Thompson

DURING THE GREAT DEPRESSION, the most notorious person in Pemiscot County was John Barnes Thompson. He was six feet tall but seemed larger because he was very broad and had such big arms and legs. He didn't have what you could call a pot belly; instead, his whole front rounded out from his chin to his thighs, like Alfred Hitchcock's profile.

Mr. Thompson owned much land and many farms all over the county. He lived in a fine brick home in Steele, not too far from where I was raised. My Uncle Will was overseer for one of his larger farms of several hundred acres just out from Cooter, where I earned my summer money by carrying water to the field hands, so I was privileged to see this legend for myself quite often. He always drove a big new car and almost always wore a blue and white striped suit. He usually smelled of whiskey; word was that he drank an awful lot, though no one ever saw him drunk or even drinking.

Mr. Thompson had earned a pretty fearsome reputation as the sheriff of Pemiscot County for a good number of years. I had heard people talk about how good he was at keeping law and order. Uncle Charlie, who had opinions about everything, told me Mr. Thompson had been a mean and tough sheriff, known for pistol-whipping bad people instead of shooting them. "Yessirree, I've heard tell how he'd whup them poor suckers with pistol butts till they wished he would shoot them and get it over with," Uncle Charlie drawled, "but he never shot anyone." I never knew how much of this was true, but I did know that most people were genuinely afraid of him, and that no one ever gave him any trouble.

What I remember most about Mr. Thompson, though, is his reputation for testing people and rewarding them if they met his standards. He was a tough teacher—I guess because he taught about life, and life is tough. When I was just a small boy, I heard people tell how he taught all of his sons to face the world. When each son was about three years old, he would stand him on a seven-foot-high hay platform in the barnyard and instruct him to dive off into daddy's arms. When Mr. Thompson judged the time was right, usually when the child was about five, he would step back just as the child jumped and let him hit the ground. Then he would say to his hurt and startled son, "It's good to trust people, but trust them only so far." I think he must have planned these final sessions around a good, soft manure pile, because he never lost a child as far as I know. His sons all rose from this indignity to become shrewd, successful businessmen.

I, too, was tested by Mr. Thompson, and although his tests did not result in my becoming shrewd, they probably did help to mold me into a more persevering soul. The first challenge came one midsummer day when Mr. Thompson was paying off the field hands at the big farm where Uncle Will was overseer. They were behind with the cotton chopping, and the hands had worked a half a day that Saturday morning in spite of the hundred degree heat to try and catch up. Mr. Thompson had brought with him his two grandsons, my friends Toby and John Barnes "Doolie" Thompson, who lived at Steele. All three of us were ten years old, born within five months of one another. Upon their arrival, we went to play in the barnyard, and soon Toby and Doolie were arguing over who claimed the mules.

"I claim the red mules because I won the cotton picking contest last fall," Doolie announced. Doolie always claimed the young strong red mules, Daisy and May, and let Toby claim the gray mules, Kate and Meg. They always relegated the pitiful old black mules, Sue and Sal, to me.

But this time Toby wouldn't stand for second best. "You didn't win that contest; I did! And I claim the red mules my own self!" he shouted.

"You didn't pick near as much cotton as me," Doolie said. "Your cotton was wet so the scales couldn't give a true weight."

"My cotton wasn't any wetter than yours was. I won the contest fair and square and I claim the red mules," Toby said.

We kept walking as they argued and eventually got in front of the house where Mr. Thompson was paying off the hands. "Grandaddy," Doolie whined, "don't I claim the red mules because I picked the best cotton last fall?"

"You didn't pick the best cotton; I did!" Toby shouted.

This bickering went on until finally Mr. Thompson turned to my Uncle Will and said with a touch of aggravation in his deep voice, "Mr. Wray, get these three boys each a good sharp hoe."

We all knew immediately that he was planning another test. Toby and Doolie calmed down for a few minutes. After a while Doolie ventured to ask, "What are we going to do, Grandaddy?"

"We are going to settle this problem of who is the best farm worker once and for all as soon as Mr. Wray brings us some hoes," he said without looking back at us as we followed him to his big gray car. "Alvin Junior will be in this challenge, too," he added.

Uncle Will returned with the implements of our little war, and Toby quickly said, "I don't have a hat."

"Mr. Wray, find this boy a hat."

We three boys went to the pump house to drink as the fields hands filed past us on their way home because it was too hot for them to work that afternoon. I could tell that Toby was drinking too much. I had learned from the hands that it wasn't good to drink very much. I drank straight from the pump what I thought was the proper amount. Mr. Thompson called out for us to get in the car, and we rode a mile due south to the back forty.

When we got there, Mr. Thompson got out of the car and looked around wisely. He made some marks with his heel on the dusty road that ran perpendicular to the cotton rows, setting off three groups of eight rows each. The rows were just a little less than a half a mile long. "Now, boys, who's got what it takes to chop cotton on a good hot day?" Nobody claimed anything as he eyed us without a trace of a smile. "Alvin, you take the first group of rows; Doolie, you take the second, and Toby will take the last. You should have just enough time to finish by sundown. The first one of you to finish, if you've chopped the cotton clean and right and good, can claim the red mules."

"But it's too hot to chop cotton, Grandaddy," Toby whined.

"You can go back to the house with me if you don't have what it takes, Toby." Mr. Thompson looked back at us as he opened his car door and added, "There will also be a twenty-dollar bill given to the best chopper."

He waited for that to sink in on us. Twenty dollars was as much as I earned in eight full weeks of carrying water to the field hands. We just stood there trying to fathom getting that much money at one time. At least I did.

"If you boys want to get done before sundown, you'd better get started," he said to break our daze. He waited a few more minutes and watched as we each took a hoe and started chopping. When we had gotten pretty far down our first rows, he called out, "See you boys about sundown, and we'll see how well you do."

Toby yelled back, "Grandaddy, I still think it's too hot to chop cotton." Mr. Thompson just got in the car and drove down the road.

Doolie immediately started chopping faster than both of us. After about twenty minutes, he was at least thirty yards out front. Just before we got to the end of our first row, Toby called out, "Doolie, my stomach hurts."

"It'll be all right, Toby; keep choppin'," Doolie called back as he started down his second row.

A few minutes later, Toby said, "My stomach hurts real bad and I feel like I'm gonna throw up."

"You've gotta keep choppin' or I'm gonna get to claim the red mules," Doolie answered, breathless from his frantic pace that had slowed considerably. It was very still and probably several degrees over a hundred, but I had been carrying water in the fields for seven weeks and was conditioned to the heat. I knew they were in greater pain than I was.

Nothing else was said. The next time we looked up, we saw Toby with his hoe on his shoulder, cutting out across the field back to Uncle Will's house. After a few minutes, Doolie, who was still pretty far ahead of me, called back, "Alvin, don't you think we ought to go check on Toby?"

"No, he's all right," I said. To myself, I said, "I'm not about to quit now."

When we were halfway through our fourth rows, Doolie said, "Alvin, don't you think we better go? Toby could really be sick. They may have to carry him to the doctor."

Without looking up from my row, I said, "You can go if you want to, but I'm gonna keep choppin'."

Doolie didn't say anything more after that, but a little while later, I looked up and saw him with his hoe on his shoulder, walking across the field toward the house. I was now more determined than ever to finish. When the heat became almost unbearable, I just closed my eyes, called up the image of that twenty-dollar bill, and reminded myself how many hot days I'd have to carry water to earn that. When I got to the back side of row five, I did have to stop to rest a while, and I realized how tired I was and how quiet it had gotten. I guess it was too hot for the crickets to rub their legs together. I looked up and saw hazy clouds forming in the west and couldn't tell how close it was to sundown. The clouds hadn't relieved the heat any. It was that kind of humid, suffocating heat that felt like someone's sweaty hand clamped over my face.

On row six, I was a little anxious because it was getting darker, and I began to think about mad dogs and how difficult it would be to run from one through the cotton when I couldn't see. And a blue racer would be harder to detect now and might even be well up my pants leg before I had a chance to hack it to pieces with my hoe. The sky was pretty, though. It was gray-blue up high but had turned a rich lilac color in the west. I guessed it was almost sundown, but couldn't be sure because the sun was hidden behind the summer haze.

When I reached the road and turned back on row seven, I started to worry that Mr. Thompson had forgotten about me. It got darker and darker, and halfway up the row, I had almost made up my mind to quit and start toward the house. Just then I saw Mr. Thompson's car lights bumping down the road in the dusk. He honked several times, and I made my way down the row to the road. When I got close to the car, he leaned his head out the window and said, "Boy, you really want that twenty dollars, don't you?"

"Yes, sir, " I said, "but I only got halfway through row seven."

"That's good enough," he said and smiled a little. "Get in the car." As we rode down the narrow road, he told me that he had carried Toby and Doolie back to Steele, thinking I would quit and walk back to the house soon after they did. Aunt Annie had called him to say I was still out there. She probably thought I had died of heat stroke or snake bite. He let me out at the house and said he'd settle up with me the next payday.

The following Saturday, Mr. Thompson called me over to his car and handed me a dollar and a half for carrying water three days—it had rained two days that week. Then he reached in his pocket purse and pulled out a crisp twenty-dollar bill. "Here's your reward for winning the challenge," he said and smiled. Then he reached in his purse again and asked, "Have you ever seen one of these?" He was holding a one-hundred-dollar bill.

"No, sir," I said, staring at it.

He let me hold it a while and said, "Alvin, if you can tell me you haven't drunk or smoked on the day you graduate from high school, I'll give you a hundred-dollar bill just like this."

"I'll sure do that, Mr. Thompson," I replied, and I meant it.

Back at Memphis the following years, I suffered difficult times in dark alleys with Cyrus Quillen and Matt McMinn and some of my other tough friends who all tried to make me smoke or take a drink of whiskey. But I never did. When I'd see Mr. Thompson on trips back to visit Uncle Will and Aunt Annie, he'd often remind me of my challenge, and I'd give him good reports.

Then, when I was fifteen, news came from the Bootheel that John Barnes Thompson had died. My mother said he died of too much whiskey. I felt really bad for a while, and, of course, I never got my hundred-dollar bill. Still, I came to appreciate his hand in steering me clear of unhealthful substances with the promise of something more tangible than Aunt Annie's preachments on bad habits, immorality, and the Day of Judgment. I still think of Mr. Thompson and sometimes smile on hot, hazy summer days, especially when there's a rich lilac sunset.

5

The Little Woman in Black

NEAR MIDSUMMER WHEN I was ten, I ventured again along the straight roads past the flat fields to my grandmother's house, which was now five miles south of Tyler. Unlike Aunt Annie and Uncle Will, who had raised my father, my mother's people were the moving kind, following work around the county. I arrived late in the afternoon to find all the menfolks gone way up in the upper part of the county to cut wood for the winter. They always did this between cotton chopping and picking. Aunt Virginia had gone to visit her sister Mary, who had moved up near Portageville, and only my grandmother was there with Jessie.

I was a little disappointed to find Jessie there. She was known as a downright mean person who made life miserable for all those around her. I never knew her relationship to the family, but thought it strange that we called her just plain "Jessie" since all of us children always called any kind of kin "aunt" or "uncle."

Jessie was a large woman who looked to have some Indian blood—but not much, because Indians don't grow hair on their faces, and Jessie had a reddish-brown mustache. Uncle Charlie said she used to shave it in her younger years. She pulled her black hair back in a knot and wore dark dresses that hung over her hulking form like a drape over a casket. She kept a dip of snuff in her lip and was forever going to the door and spitting long distances. Uncle Charlie said she even chewed tobacco. She always brought her cigarette-making machine and Bugler tobacco with her. I remember one visit when she and the men sat around and made cigarettes all afternoon.

Jessie was old but not as old as grandmother, and I guess had never had any children; if she did have any, she never mentioned them. She made no bones about not liking kids. Once, when someone at grandmother's remarked that children should be seen and not heard, she barked, "Children should be neither seen nor heard."

Jessie liked to gamble about as much as she disliked being around children. Although the menfolks didn't like her, I've seen them take off two days work while she was visiting just to play poker, with her cussing and dealing and spitting all the while.

Jessie is the only person I ever knew who could intimidate my grandmother. I never saw anyone Jessie *didn't* intimidate. The bad thing about it was that she intimidated Grandmother right out of her tradition of making tea cookies for me. When I got there this time, I asked if she had any. She said, in a bit of a stew, "I'll see if I have time to make some," whereupon Jessie shouted, "There you go, spoiling that child! We won't have time to bake tea cookies this week." They had dishpans full of blackberries all over the kitchen, making jelly or something.

I stayed outside as much as I could, making up chores to do around the barn and outbuildings to stay away from Jessie.

Late that afternoon, I sat on the front porch that faced due south and thought once again how this was probably the most barren and desolate part of the whole Bootheel. This section had been cleared of almost all trees, and it seemed you could see forever and ever. The only thing that broke up the almost desert-like view was a quarter-mile stretch of brush and willow trees out in the field straight south from the house. The men called that pitiful little oasis "the Dead Ditch." Years ago when the entire Bootheel was swamp, ditches were dug to drain the land. Most of them had since been filled in, but this one was left for some reason. It was dry in the summer.

On previous visits, I had heard the men talking on Grandmother's front porch about the Dead Ditch and a wild chicken that had lived at least three years there amid the brush and willows. They knew some people who had seen it venture out on the edge of the cotton fields, but it would hasten back to the Dead Ditch on seeing them. They said Uncle T.L. had taken his rifle down there to shoot it one time, but my grandmother had told him, "Let that chicken be." My grandmother and her people believed in haints and saints and the sanctity of private things.

The next morning after breakfast, I went out to pump water till the troughs ran over. Since all the mules were gone for the day and I couldn't make up any more chores to stay out of the house, I began to mull over plans I had made the night before to catch the wild chicken. I had seen a Frank Buck movie in which they caught wild animals in Africa with traps, so I began to put together my own Bootheel version with a small washtub, several ears of corn, and a ball of twine. It was a hot August day, and the dust burned through the soles of my shoes as I hauled my paraphernalia down to the Dead Ditch. I'd do anything to get out of the house and away from Jessie.

I was most mindful of the possible presence of blue racers as I made my way down into the ditch, which was about eight feet deep, twenty-five feet wide, and bone dry. When I found a spot relatively clear of weeds, I propped up the washtub with a stick, tied the twine to the bottom of the stick, and pulled the twine almost as far as it would go into the brush, where I could hide and watch. Then I shucked an ear of corn and rubbed the kernels off, making a trail several feet out from the tub with a little pile of kernels just inside the tub. I went back into the brush to hold the end of the twine while I waited.

An hour later, I had just about given up when I thought I heard a clucking sound. Sure enough, out strutted a nice-looking Rhode Island Red hen. Very slowly she started eating the corn; it seemed forever before she got close to the tub. When she did, she was obviously wary of how this free lunch might end up. She stopped, looked at the tub, went around and around it, and finally got brave enough to stretch her neck and pick the kernels out from under it without walking into the trap. Finally, in desperation, I pulled the twine, hoping to land the edge of the tub on her neck, but the noise scared her and she was five feet away before it even fell. I rigged the whole thing up again and waited till the sun was noon high, but she never came back.

I hauled my stuff back to Grandmother's house and washed up for dinner. While we ate great helpings of chicken and dumplings, string beans, and green tomato chowchow, Grandmother asked what I'd been doing.

"I've been down in the Dead Ditch trying to catch the wild chicken," I said.

"I don't know why you'd want to bother that chicken. What would you do with it if you caught it?"

"I thought I could just put it up with the pen chickens out back."

"That wild chicken couldn't live penned up any longer than I could live in Memphis."

Nothing more was said about the wild chicken.

After dinner, I sat on the porch swing and watched a hummingbird. If I sat still enough, I could feel an occasional breeze. But the breezes were faint and far between, so I ventured in and interrupted Jessie's continuous talking to tell Grandmother I was going to walk to the Tyler store to get an RC Cola and a Moon Pie. It was a hot five miles into Tyler, but the prospect of reaching into the ice water to pull an RC out of the cold drink chest at the store was inviting enough to warrant the trip.

I cut diagonally across the fields of cotton, hay, and corn. The sun burned through my hat, but I didn't mind because it was a friendly warmth that seemed to effuse my brain with the wonderful, eerie space of the Bootheel.

After about forty-five minutes of unhurried walking, I was two and a half miles into a large hay field when I saw a little black spot coming toward me. I walked curiously on, and as the spot got nearer, I could see it was a tiny lady dressed all in black, probably about seventy-five years old. She was perhaps five feet tall and took little bitty steps toward me. As we got within proper speaking distance of each other, she said in a slightly shaky voice, "Hello, young man." Her wrinkled face cracked into a smile.

"Howdy, ma'am," I returned politely.

"Young man, do you know where Elmer Johnson lives? That's my brother. I haven't seen him in more than thirty years now. I know I'm not a-going to live too much longer, so I left Humboldt, Tennessee, three days ago to find him. Got some nice rides in trucks and wagons, and they let me cross the ferry at Cottonwood Point. All I know is that my brother lives on this side of the river. Last I heard of him, he lived somewhere out from Tyler."

"I'm sorry, ma'am, but I've never heard of that name, and I don't think there are any people around here for miles except in Tyler."

"Well, I thank you just the same. I talked to some folks in Tyler, and they told me they'd heard tell of someone around Red Town who might be Elmer. They said the best way to get to Red Town was right straight through these here fields, so I guess I'll just keep on going till I get somewhere. God bless you, son."

With that, she turned and went on across the great hay field. I turned around and walked backwards to watch her, and she got smaller and smaller until she just kind of disappeared in the summer haze.

I went on into Tyler and got my RC and Moon Pie, but the usual joy of that indulgence was dampened somewhat by the thought of the little lady walking out there somewhere in the desolate heat. I barely got back to Grandmother's house before dark and was still wondering about her as we ate supper. I told Grandmother and Jessie. Jessie, of course, paid no attention at all to me. Grandmother said nothing, but I did notice she looked intently at me as I described the little woman out there in the open fields trying to find her brother.

The next morning, there were still no tea cookies in sight, so I made up some excuse to walk halfway across the county to my Aunt Annie's house. I stayed there several weeks, worrying every so often about the little old woman in black.

Not long before it was time for school to start, my mother came from Memphis to collect me. We stopped at Grandmother's house to spend the night before going back to the city. Jessie was gone, and Grandmother was making big, round, crisp, golden tea cookies within an hour of my arrival.

That night at the supper table, someone brought up the subject of my trying to catch the wild chicken down at the Dead Ditch with a washtub. It brought quite a bit of laughter, and Uncle T.L. said, "I'm gonna take my rifle and shoot that damn chicken yet."

"You leave that chicken alone, T.L," Grandmother said sternly. "You let that chicken be."

Everyone was quiet until Grandpa Pete asked, "What's this about you seeing a little woman in the fields a while back?"

I guess Grandmother had said something to him about it. Everyone listened as I told again in detail exactly what happened. Again there was a little silence.

"I've been over to Red Town twice lately," Uncle Charlie said, "and no one has ever seen or heard of any little woman in black." He paused a moment. "And no one has ever known of anyone ever living in these parts named Elmer Johnson."

They all looked at me as if I had maybe seen a haint, so I didn't say anything more.

When I went to visit my grandparents the following summer, they had moved again. Now they were a about a mile north of Tyler, away from that barren place. One day, as Grandmother boiled laundry in a big black pot in the back yard, I asked her about the wild chicken in the Dead Ditch. She looked at me funny and said that, as far as she knew, it was still down there when they left. I wanted to ask—but didn't—about the little woman in black. To this day, when I travel in my mind to the Bootheel, she's still there, like that wary chicken, walking somewhere through the vast expanse of corn, cotton, and hay to find her brother.

6

The River Revivalist

IT WAS AUGUST, MY favorite month. Bugs sing the loudest in August, the sun beats down the hottest, jumping in the swimming hole is the funnest, dirt roads are the dustiest, and lemonade is the wettest in August.

I had been staying with Aunt Annie for a while. There were no other kids there, but I kept busy at my summer job of carrying buckets of water to the field hands. I earned fifty cents a day doing this—pretty good spending money for a ten-year-old during the Depression.

When the crops were laid by and my job petered out, I decided I needed a change of pace. Daddy came by on one of his forays into the county farms to make someone an unrefusable deal on a truck from his car dealership in nearby Steele, which was about the largest of the small towns in that area of the Bootheel. I told him I was ready to leave Aunt Annie's, so he carried me across the county about about eight miles south to Uncle Virgil's place, about half a mile from the Mississippi River and almost to Arkansas.

Our relatives' houses were usually called by the aunts' names, but for some reason this one was Uncle Virgil's, not Aunt Minnie's. Uncle Virgil never talked much, but he always smiled and hugged me when I arrived and then rarely paid any more attention to me as I blended in with the rest of the crowd. There were twelve children all living at home, plus other visitors forever wandering about the house, sleeping in lofts and on screened porches. Aunt Minnie always made a big fuss over me because I brought news from the rest of the relatives and from Mama in Memphis.

Two of Uncle Virgil's children, Wanda and J.I., were about my age and were my special playmates. We'd finish our chores quickly so we could go down by the river and look for tommy toes or fish for crawdads or spit on straws that we would then carefully lower into holes in the ground and pull up to find long doodlebugs magically dangling from our spittle. But the ultimate fun was riding in a little cart pulled by Aunt Minnie's goat.

Daddy got me there in time for dinner—fried field corn, cucumbers and red onions in sweetened vinegar water, stewed okra that slid down easy, fried chicken, mashed potatoes and gravy, biscuits and honey, and cobbler made from Aunt Minnie's canned dewberries. Later that afternoon, when Wanda, J.I., and I had just entered the throes of ecstasy with the goat cart, Aunt Minnie hollered out the back door.

"We'll have to finish supper early if we're going to make it to Tyler in time for preachin' tonight, so ya'll better start on your evenin' chores."

I had not planned on going to church in the middle of the week. I was used to Bible reading every night at Aunt Annie's, but at least there I didn't have to sit on a hard pew for two hours. I had never been to one of these revivals, though, and was a little curious. Aunt Minnie was excited about seeing the famous preacher who was holding the meeting. He was one of those high-powered river revivalists who traveled up and down the Mississippi, stopping at congregations near its dusty banks to give farm families a dose of religious zeal.

After supper, the women and children got in a big wagon pulled by a team of mules, and the men walked. I rode some and walked some, not wanting to miss anything in either group. Only two cars passed us the whole way.

As we approached Tyler, the white Baptist church building with its proper steeple stood out against the pink sky and dominated the flat land. It was the only two-story building in town.

We filed in and took up two and a half pews. When the choir began to sing, so did the rest of the congregation because all the songs were old ones that everybody knew. Wanda, J.I., and I sang at the tops of our lungs, knowing that we wouldn't be allowed to make a peep when the preaching started. After about six songs, the choir members sat down to be exhorted with the rest of us, and we children began to draw pictures and play quiet church games.

After a while, when we had run out of ways to have fun without making noise, I got overwhelmed with some very loud, convincing preaching. I looked up and found I could not look away from the athletic-looking preacher, whose square, clean-shaven face beaded with sweat as the farmers' wives cooled their sleeping babies with cardboard fans from the funeral home.

He was talking about how things might happen when Jesus would come again and start Judgment Day. That day would no doubt be soon, he said, because people had gotten so sinful the Lord was surely about to get enough of it. Of course, no man knoweth the hour, he quoted, but all the Biblical signs pointed to the time we were living in.

He went on to describe in detail the last day as he imagined it—with lots of scriptures to give his imagination credence. And the day he imagined was only five days away! It would still be August, I thought. Surely Jesus wouldn't come before vacation was over! As I worried over this possibility, the preacher's booming voice broke back into my thoughts with more details.

I got a little more uncomfortable when he came to "the sound of the trump—a sound that will be heard 'round the world." He talked about how happy he and his wife and child would be when they were caught up in the air to meet Jesus, who would be descending in a cloud. And he talked about the fear and remorse his poor drunken brother would feel when he heard the trumpet and knew he was not prepared to go.

Then he went into a terrifying description of Hell—the Lake of Fire, Gehenna, where the worm dieth not, the eternal place of torment for all liars, fornicators, thieves, and revellers (a Biblical term defined by preachers as "those who went to dances"). I began to heat up a little right then as I evaluated my actions of the past few weeks and wondered whether I was in danger.

As he built up to the invitation, he reminded the sweating congregation that we all have sinned, and only by giving our lives to Jesus could we avoid eternal damnation. He even called out some names of people who needed to come forward—a trick I had never seen in regular Sunday services. This man had done his homework and was prepared to bring in the sheaves.

I was almost too weak to stand as the congregation rose and the choir started singing "When the trumpet of the Lord shall sound, and time shall be no more...." About thirty people went forward, including several of Uncle Virgil's older kids, while the preacher stood beside the pulpit with outstretched arms, shouting exhortations above the strains of the excited singers.

I decided I was too young to get involved in something this serious. I had heard Aunt Annie, by far the most religious of my aunts, mention the age of accountability the last time I was there. She had explained that this age is different with different people, depending on when they realize they have sinned and need a savior. She said it was usually around twelve. I wasn't aware of any dark sins in my life, and since I wasn't even quite eleven yet, I decided to stay put with Wanda and J.I.

But when they passed the collection plate, I was sufficiently moved to put in fifty cents. I had brought two and a half dollars with me—a whole week's wages—to impress my cousins, who never had any money.

I was anxious to get back outside, thinking that a long ride home in the wagon would surely put everybody back into a more playful spirit. I was severely disappointed. Once we were on the road, Aunt Minnie commenced to rehash the whole sermon. She went on and on about how she certainly agreed with that wonderful river revivalist that the end of the world must be just around the corner.

I didn't sleep too well that night. The next morning, after five biscuits with chocolate gravy plus eggs and side meat, I began to think seriously about what the rest of the week was going to be like. I didn't savor the prospect of stopping play early every day to go be scared out of my wits and end up putting my whole two and half dollars in the collection plate. I decided to go back to Aunt Annie's before it was everlastingly too late.

"Now, Alvin Junior, that's an awful long way for you to walk in this heat all by yourself," Aunt Minnie said when I told her I was leaving.

"I can make it all right; I know where the water pump is on the way," I told her.

She gave me a sack of tea cakes when she realized I was determined to go, and I left about mid-morning. Wanda and J.I. walked with me down to the main dirt road that led north, where I struck off by myself on the eight-mile journey to Aunt Annie's.

There were few houses along the road, and only one car passed me as I made my way toward the first turn at Number Eight. From there it was a straight three miles to the next turn.

The desolate road was covered with a fine, soft, powdery dust that bore the undisturbed tracks of snakes and worms and small creatures that had scurried across it unseen, and again I could hear the preacher's words, "where the worm dieth not." Sometimes I heard a rustle in the ditch above the steady hum of summer bugs. I wasn't afraid of most creatures, but as I stepped over these tracks I began to think about the two things I did fear—mad dogs and blue racer snakes.

My wise friend Martha Sue had tried to tell me earlier that blue racers weren't as fast as everybody said, and that mad dogs couldn't catch someone who could really run. She was the only person I knew who believed that. As these ominous thoughts gathered, I was bothered by some guilt about leaving Uncle Virgil's so I wouldn't have to go to church every night. I felt pretty deceitful about ducking out that way. The sun burned through my straw hat, and I thought about the liars in the Lake of Fire.

Suddenly a long, loud, frightening sound like nothing I'd ever heard blasted across the land. I walked on; in about two minutes, I heard it again and by this time was convinced that it must be the trumpet of the Lord. The third time I heard the blast, it seemed much closer. I turned to look back down the road and saw a billowing cloud of dust rolling toward me. I thought the preacher had said the cloud would come from the sky, but this had to be it: the world was coming to an end. I wished hard to be at Aunt Annie's. She was so good and prayed so much, I thought maybe they'd let me go with her to Heaven.

I jumped across the ditch into a hay field to wait for my fate. I heard the sound two more times before I saw a huge black and yellow box through the clouds of dust coming toward me. I hadn't heard the preacher mention a black and yellow box, but then I hadn't listened to the first part of his sermon, either. Maybe he had described a gigantic cart that was supposed to gather up the sinners while the good people were being caught up in the sky with Jesus.

As the box got closer, I could see it was bigger than anything that had ever been on any road in Pemiscot County or even in Memphis. I squatted in the hay and watched. As it passed by, I saw the words "JENKINS' ROLLING STORE" in giant red letters on its side.

I basked in relief for a few minutes while the dust settled, and then I went on down the road. When I had gone about a mile, I saw the box stopped at a crossroad with some women and children gathered around it. I stopped to gawk a while, and a man in a plaid suit gave me a peppermint stick.

When I got to Aunt Annie's, she told me this was the first year the Rolling Store had come through Pemiscot County. The big box, a common sight in the Bootheel and northeast Arkansas during the thirties and forties, was built over a big truck frame. It would park at some isolated corner for half a day so farm families could get groceries and things without having to make the long trip to a town store. It announced its arrival with that horrible horn—a combination foghorn and siren.

I never saw the Rolling Store again that summer, but I heard the screeching horn far away on the country roads.

One day, I was helping Aunt Annie snap beans on the back porch when we heard the horn perhaps three or four miles away.

"Is that anything like the sound we'll hear on Judgment Day that the revival man preached about?"

"Lordy, no," Aunt Annie replied. "That sound will be more of a heavenly sound. And believe me, Alvin Junior," she added, "the time is surely near."

None of this helped me go to sleep at night in the far back bedroom. One middle of the night, I was almost sure I heard the sound of a horn far off in the distance. As I lay there waiting and listening, I knew there were more things in life to fear right along with mad dogs and blue racer snakes.

7

The Flood

ONE SATURDAY A FEW days after Halloween in 1936, my mother called me into the living room for a serious talk. "Your father," she began, "has decided that it's best you go and live with him in the Bootheel." When she got that far, she burst into tears and could not fully explain. Finally she got control of herself and made a little speech about how she and Daddy had made this plan for me, but still I couldn't glean any real reason from it.

While she talked and cried, I wondered if this could have anything to do with Mr. Ellison. Mother had met him since we had moved to Memphis. I was only ten years old, but I could tell he was interested in marrying Mother, even though she and Daddy were still married. She finished her speech and said she knew I would understand. I didn't understand, and I had mixed feelings about leaving Mother, but I wasn't all *that* upset because the Missouri Bootheel was the greatest place in the world to me.

So, after Sunday dinner the next day, Mr. Ellison came in his car, and he and Mother carried me down to the Greyhound bus station. Mother sobbed into her handkerchief as they loaded my very small suitcase and small cardboard box; then she hugged me in tears just before I climbed in. As the bus pulled out, Mr. Ellison smiled and waved and Mother kept crying. I felt a little like crying myself, but I thought about the fun I usually had in the Bootheel and soon got over it.

As we crossed the Harahan Bridge over the Mississippi River, people on the bus were talking about the high water. It had already rained a lot that fall. The river was out of its banks, and the water was up very high on the levee on the Arkansas side. As we followed Highway 61 up the west side of the river, we could see water in all the cotton rows, making strange diagonal patterns all over the land. In many places the water was over the cotton—acres and acres of water, creating lakes I had never seen before.

Halfway to Missouri it started raining. For some reason my mother had bought my ticket to Steele, where I was born. I had not quite figured that out because my daddy lived in Caruthersville. I got off at the Steele bus depot just after dark, got my very small suitcase and small cardboard box, and sat on a bench inside and waited about an hour before Daddy arrived. When he drove up, I rushed out and he hugged me, but he didn't hug me quite right. We put my box and suitcase in the back of the car and got in to leave. But, instead of turning toward Caruthersville, he turned the car back south toward Cooter. I didn't say anything.

"I haven't been able to work things out in Caruthersville, so I'm going to let you stay with Mrs. Pet and go to school in Cooter." There was a moment of silence. I had never heard of Mrs. Pet, but I didn't say anything.

"At least," he said, "until I can work things out." I sat and wondered what this was all about as we drove through the four miles of darkness to Cooter. It was still raining, and my daddy carefully maintained his speed to keep from getting stuck in the muddy ruts.

Just before we got to the little town, I ventured to ask why I couldn't stay with Aunt Annie and Uncle Will. "The water's gotten so high that they can't get the water out of the fields, so Aunt Annie and Uncle Will have gone over to Tennessee," he said. "You know your Aunt Annie has always been afraid of high water." He paused and then added, "Anyway, even if they were at home, it would be too far for you to walk to school."

It took no time for us to reach the edge of town, where we turned off on a very dark little road to the left. Cooter had a population of about two hundred, and there wasn't much there except the school, the post office, a gas station, a store or two, and a fine home that belonged to Dr. Cooper, who was one of very few doctors in Pemiscot County and the only one most people would see. Electricity had not made it to Cooter then, and the clouded, moonless night was like the inside of a wet, deep mine shaft.

We turned down another yet narrower road, and before we came to the last house, Daddy told me that Mrs. Pet was a widow lady and that her son, who made deliveries for the coal company in Steele, lived with her. We got my things out and walked up to the porch by the yellow light of the lamp that shone faintly from the front room. We knocked, and there was Mrs. Pet. Daddy introduced me, and she was warm enough but rather serious. She looked to be about my grandmother's age, but it was hard to tell because the all-purpose living and eating room had only one lamp and everything—even she—seemed dark gray.

I suppose Daddy had already made arrangements with her, because she seemed to be expecting me. Then everything happened so fast. Daddy called her over to the side and gave her some money. He turned and said, "I'll see you in a week or so when I get things worked out. You go on to school tomorrow. Everything will be fine." In a moment he was in his car and gone.

Mrs. Pet walked quietly across the room and opened a door to a darker room facing south, a bedroom with a big bed in the middle and a small bed over to the side of the room. "You will sleep in the little bed," she said. She lit a lamp and I could see what else was in the barren room: a makeshift dresser, raw wooden floors, and one small single window. I put my suitcase and box down by my appointed bed and went back into the front room to sit down, but Mrs. Pet motioned for me to follow her as she showed me the rest of the house. The side room to the north was just for storage, with canned goods and groceries on shelves. The back porch had a washstand out in the open with two wash pans and a big long white towel hanging beside it. She pointed to the wooden walk that led to the outhouse, and it was black back there and still misting rain. It didn't take long to see what there was to see. Then we went back in and just sat.

Mrs. Pet was a pleasant lady, but she just sat. And I just sat because I had been taught to speak when spoken to. I waited for her conversation but it didn't come. After forty-five minutes of sitting, I said, "My daddy said you have a son who delivers coal."

"Yes, Rupert is my only boy. He helps take care of me. He delivers coal. He usually doesn't get home till quite late. Some nights he stays over with my sister Rose because the roads are so bad and he works so late."

We sat in silence some more. I picked up an old newspaper and read a little, but not much because the paper was three months old. After a while, Mrs. Pet said, "When you get ready to go to bed, go ahead on."

I went to the back porch, lit the lantern, and ventured out into the blackness to the outhouse. Back at the washstand, I dipped my hands in what felt like freezing water, touched them to my face, and dried quickly. Then I told Mrs. Pet good night, went in the bedroom, and closed the door. It was so dark I couldn't even see how to get to my little bed, so I opened the door again to get my bearings and pushed it back, leaving just a crack to let in some light. After I went to bed, she closed the door again and it was pitch black all around me. I had never been afraid of the dark, but I had never really loved it. I lay there under a rough, clean sheet and a thin quilt, thinking that it seemed only a few minutes ago I had been in Memphis with steam heat and running water.

I did go to sleep, though. After some time, I heard a big truck roar up and supposed it was Rupert. I could hear Mrs. Pet saying things to him, but I didn't hear him answer. In a few minutes, the door opened and closed again, and in darkness I heard the dropping of shoes and clothing. Then I went back to sleep.

It was still dark when Mrs. Pet opened the door and called Rupert and me for breakfast. Rupert didn't get right up; I did. I went out back to wash my face and returned to the front room that had, besides a pot-bellied coal stove, a wood stove for cooking in the corner and a little table for eating. I guess Mrs. Pet had slept there somewhere, but I saw no sign of a cot or pallet.

All the food smelled good, and I began to cheer up a little. I went over and said good morning to Mrs. Pet; she looked at me as if that were an unusual thing for a person to do, and then she returned my greeting. I sat down to a table of side meat, fried potatoes, gravy, a big plate of biscuits, and a fruit jar full of sorghum. The morning was starting off fine.

Rupert came in, and we sat quietly and ate. Rupert's hands and face looked permanently dark from coal dust. After a while, Mrs. Pet said, "Junior…"

Since she paused in her naturally slow speech, I felt it wasn't being impolite to tell her immediately that folks in Memphis called me Alvin, and I liked that better.

"Well," she said without seeming to have heard me, "the Thompsons and Doolie moved down a little ways from here about two months ago. You might go down and go to school with him."

"Doolie lives here now?"

"Yes, they moved from Steele for some reason."

About thirty minutes before I figured school would start, Mrs. Pet pointed toward the Thompson house from the front porch, and I walked the quarter-mile down the road and knocked on the door. Doolie's mother was surprised to see me.

"Alvin Junior! What are you doing here?"

"Mother and Daddy decided I should live with Daddy now, but Daddy's getting things worked out in Caruthersville, so he carried me over here to stay with Mrs. Pet and go to the Cooter school for a while."

"You mean you've living down there with Mrs. Pet?"

"Yes, ma'am." I could tell she thought this was a strange situation.

Just then Doolie and his little sister ran into the room, and in a few minutes we were heading down the road to the Cooter school. It was on the opposite end of town, but town was only a quarter of a mile long. We walked through a gray mist, and our shoes were soon wet as we passed three little stores—two of which were boarded up—a filling station, and a gin that didn't seem to be operating at the time. When we got to the school, Doolie took me in to meet the principal and told him I was a new student for the fifth grade. The principal asked me some questions for a form and took me to the fifth and sixth grade room. There were only thirteen or fourteen students there.

The teacher was nice enough, but she didn't seem to know anything. I was a little surprised that no one seemed to think it unusual to have a new kid sitting in class. We just sat there and talked. Doolie said the combined classes usually had about thirty kids, "but a lot of people have moved out for fear of high water." Out the window, we could see water standing in the low places.

Not long before lunch, we had a spelling bee. Even though I was only an average speller, I was outspelling everyone and starting to feel pretty smart. Then again, maybe everybody that had any sense had already left town.

I walked back to Mrs. Pet's for lunch and then to school again to sit for a while longer. They let school out early, about two o'clock, and we sloshed back through town. Doolie and his little sister went in their house, and I turned off on the little black, muddy road to Mrs. Pet's. As I approached her house, I really looked at it for the first time. It was just a long three-room unpainted house, weather-worn gray, with black roll roofing. There was no decoration anywhere in the yard, just a plank walkway through the water. The few trees around the house were already bare, as were all the trees I'd seen in Cooter. It was a drab and depressing place, nothing like the sun-bright Bootheel of the summers I'd spent roaming from one houseful of relatives to another.

I walked into the front room, where Mrs. Pet was sewing. She greeted me and continued to sew. And there I was.

I looked out the window for a while; it was still drizzling as it had been for two months. I piddled with some empty spools, using them with soap and rubber bands to make little things that scooted across the floor. Mrs. Pet looked at them once and grunted, but she didn't exclaim over my genius.

Time was passing very slowly. I went outside and just stood in the drizzle, but I had no idea what to do. Mrs. Pet must have seen. She called me in and took me to the side room, where she looked through some trunks and found an old pair of black boots.

"Put these on over your shoes and see if you can walk in them," she said. While I pulled them on, she looked some more and found an old gray slicker. She held it up to me and cut the arms and bottom off; it was still enormous, but I could keep it on. Then she found an old floppy rain hat and plopped it on my head. "This will keep you dry, at least," she said. "It will be about an hour before supper."

I didn't know the word *boredom,* but I knew I couldn't sit around there for another hour, so I sloshed back toward town. The only thing I found open was the filling station. I walked in and there, sitting by the stove, was a little man who looked familiar. I remembered him because my daddy had bought gasoline at the station before.

"Mr. McClure, do you remember me?" I asked. The garb I was wearing probably would have kept my own mother from recognizing me.

He peered under the hat into my half-hidden face and said, "I can't say that I do, son."

"I'm Alvin Allen's boy, Alvin Junior."

"Are you really, now!" he exclaimed. "What are you doing here this time of year?"

I told him my story.

"That's awful peculiar," he said. "But that's the way old Alvin is."

"Well, he told me I couldn't stay with Uncle Will and Aunt Annie because they have gone over to Tennessee, but I didn't have time to ask him why I couldn't stay with Grandmother or Uncle Elly or Aunt Minnie."

"I'll tell you why, son," he said. "I've sat here and watched all your kinfolks pull out for higher ground. All this rain has got people scared."

"Are you scared, Mr. McClure?"

"A little rain ain't nothin to be scared of. I'm keepin dry."

I sat by Mr. McClure's stove and talked until nearly five o'clock. Then I sloshed back to Mrs. Pet's for supper. Rupert wasn't home, but she went ahead and put out fried potatoes, beans, and cornbread. After supper, I made up games for myself and sat around and read a few things I found stacked in the corner—an old Farmers' Almanac and a religious calendar from a funeral home. It seemed a long time before I went to bed, but it couldn't have been much past eight. The night was a repeat of the one before, and the next morning we again got up and ate in silence. I put on my rain garb and dragged my feet in the big boots through the water to Doolie's house, sloshed on to school, where we sat in dullness, sloshed to the house for lunch, sloshed back to school. Every day was the same.

My only relief was Mr. McClure. I walked to his station every day after school. On the fourth day I told Mrs. Pet that I would just go there straight from school and stay until supper time. At least at Mr. McClure's I could see an occasional car stop for gas on its way to the Cottonwood Point Ferry. And he took the *St. Louis Post-Dispatch,* so I could keep up with Alley Oop, Orphan Annie, and all the others. He also had a dog named Red—a big brown mixed-breed, houndish-looking dog with a limp in his left hind leg who just lay around and looked skinny. One day, I asked Mr. McClure if Red was a friendly dog that would take to petting.

"Yeah, go on over."

So I rubbed his back, Red responded, and I made friends with him. Sometimes I could even get Mrs. Pet to put scrap food in a bag that I would take to him. If Doolie had been there, I'm sure he would have claimed Red for his own, but Doolie's family left Cooter soon after I got there. My fifth and sixth grade class was down to nine students by the second week. When I told Mr. McClure, he said, "Yeah, they're all moving west around Kennett just in case it floods like it did in twenty-nine." Then he told me about the big flood when several hundred people drowned. As he talked, he just sat and whittled and periodically shook down the coals in the stove, never seeming to be overly concerned about the weather. I figured he was a wise old man, and I took courage from his apparent lack of fear.

I went on without too much discontent in my routine: sitting in silence, sloshing to school, petting the red dog. I expected Daddy to come for me in two weeks, and I could stand anything for that long.

At the end of two weeks Daddy hadn't returned, and I said to Mr. McClure, "I wonder where my daddy is."

"Oh, your daddy takes off to far places sometimes. He might be as far up as St. Louis."

This didn't make me feel any better. Neither did all the wagons and trucks loaded with furniture that I saw going west every day. Mr. McClure explained that people were in sort of a state of panic because the water was almost lapping over the levee, and I could tell that even he had a bit of a worried look in his eye.

All the little stores in town were locked tight; the station was the only thing open. And even though school was in session, nothing was going on there—just people talking about the flood. I started losing courage fast when I heard a boy say, "If the levee does break, it'll probably break between Tyler and Cottonwood Point because that's the weakest point on the levee, my daddy says. If it breaks bad, he says there'll come a water wall that will destroy everything in its path for fifteen or twenty miles."

That afternoon I sat at the station, which was just about five miles out from the smack-dab center point between Tyler and Cottonwood Point, and told Mr. McClure what the boy had said.

"I don't think that levee's gonna break," he said, trying to comfort me.

I felt a little less comforted when he went on to say, "I tell you one thing I don't want you to do. You see that house over there with that ladder going up to the roof?"

"Yessir."

He pointed in another direction and said, "See that other house with a ladder going to the top?"

"Yessir."

"Don't you get on top of any house. Does Mrs. Pet have a ladder on her house?"

"I saw one out back."

"Don't you get on top of that house. You get fifteen feet up in a good solid tree. That *tree* won't wash down. Get in a tree and wait."

"Will I hear the water wall coming?"

"That levee's not gonna break. Don't you worry."

I left for supper not feeling a whole lot better. Besides all I'd heard that day, it had been three weeks and still no sign of Daddy. And I hadn't gotten any mail—Mother thought I was in Caruthersville, and the Cooter Post Office was closed anyway. I really began to feel sorry for myself when I realized my birthday was coming in a few days and no one even knew. Mrs. Pet and I ate more fried potatoes and beans in silence that night. I didn't believe it would be right for me to hint to her that I would be having a birthday.

The next day was Thanksgiving. Mrs. Pet had gotten a small ham, and she fried sweet instead of Irish potatoes to go with it and our beans—not at all what I was used to on a holiday. She was a good cook, but she just didn't have much to work with. Rupert was home that day, and he wandered in and out. I didn't think the station would be open, but I put on my rain gear and automatically carried myself there to find Mr. McClure opening up.

"I didn't think you'd be here today," I said, perking up.

"I didn't either, but after dinner I figured I might as well come on in. Somebody might decide to pull out today and need to fill up."

He went in to stoke the fire, and I petted Red.

"Guess how old I'll be my next birthday," I said after a while.

"Twelve."

"No, I'll be eleven in three days."

"Your birthday is the twenty-ninth?"

"That's right. I bet Daddy will be here then to take me to Caruthersville."

"Maybe so, son."

On my birthday, we sat in the station worrying about the flood. It was late afternoon, and I had decided Daddy wasn't coming for my birthday. I started looking for cars with Tennessee plates—thought maybe I could hitch a ride on one going across on the ferry to Dyersburg, and from there it was only about seventy miles to Memphis. While I formulated this plan, Mr. McClure pulled out a box and handed me a slingshot.

"Here's you a slingshot for your birthday," he said. He had carved my initials on it. I thanked him very much and went out to shoot rocks at birds on the telephone wire. This was a fine distraction, and I forgot my fears for a while.

It was about a week later that Mr. McClure told me he'd heard the ferry at Cottonwood Point wasn't running. He said his wife was giving him a lot of trouble about getting out of there and going to higher ground.

"Are you gonna go?" I asked, thinking surely he wouldn't but afraid that he might.

"I might have to close up and go."

I sloshed back to supper in the endless drizzle, wondering what in the world I would do without Mr. McClure. That night, Mrs. Pet mentioned that her sister over in some small town about thirty miles away was wanting her to come till the flood scare was past. She asked me if I wanted to go with her and Rupert if they went.

"Where's my daddy?" I blurted, confused and close to tears. "I'll have to ask him if I can go."

"I'll walk up to Mrs. Sullivan's and put in a call to your daddy to find out what's going on."

The next afternoon when I got out of school, Mr. McClure's filling station was locked up. I called for him a few times and tried not to cry. Finally I walked on to the house. Rupert's big coal truck was there, and he was loading it with furniture and supplies. Mrs. Pet said she had gotten in touch with people in Caruthersville who had gotten in touch with people in Portageville who had talked with my daddy, and he had said for me to stay there and wait for him, he would come and get me.

Rupert and Mrs. Pet got in the coal truck and left about four o'clock. She had left me some biscuits and instructions on what to do with the stove and lamp when I should leave. I sat in the front room and looked down the road. It got dark, and Daddy hadn't come. I could see one or two other lights in windows around in the darkness, so I knew there were still some people left. At eight o'clock, I made a pallet on the floor in the front room and slept off and on. I let the lamp burn all night. Earlier,

I had put a ladder up against a tree with good limbs that I could run to if I heard the wall of water.

When it got daylight again, I put three cold biscuits in a pan and set them on the coal stove. When they were warm, I sopped sorghum for breakfast. Then I put on my hat and slicker and boots. Outside, the water stood as much as six inches in places. There was very little traffic. I sloshed around downtown and didn't see a thing, so I went to the filling station and just sat on a bench out front. Two or three cars passed, going west. About ten-thirty, I started back to sop some more sorghum and saw a big truck without its trailer on the main road to Mrs. Pet's house. I tried to run in my big boots to see who it was. When I got to the truck parked out from her yard, I saw Daddy in high boots, searching the house. I hollered at him, and he told me to come to the house. I hurried up and hugged him, and this time he hugged me a little bit better.

"You thought I wasn't gonna come get you, didn't you," he joked.

"Where have you been?"

"Up north on business," he said, not looking at me. "I thought I'd be done earlier. I started out to get you yesterday, but the water was so high I had to go back and get this rig that's higher off the ground. Get your stuff and let's go."

I went in and crammed stuff in my suitcase and box and did what Mrs. Pet had told me to do with the lamp and stove. When we climbed into the truck, Daddy said, "I'm going to take you to Blytheville to stay at Aunt Lou's; it's higher ground there."

I told him everything I'd heard at school and that almost everybody had evacuated.

"That damn levee will not break," he said, disgusted. "If it doesn't stop raining, we might be under water because there's no drainage, but that levee won't break."

We rode along in the wet, gray silence of the Bootheel until we got about halfway between Cooter and the highway that went down into Arkansas to Blytheville. Then Daddy said, "Look over there." I looked off to the left and saw some pigs swimming in the water, trying to find high ground.

We got to higher ground at a small town called Yarbro and stopped at a little cafe. Daddy took me in and told the man there to feed me anything I wanted. So I ate a big plate lunch while Daddy made some business calls. He also called Aunt Lou to tell her he was bringing me in.

As we drove into Blytheville, he said, "I think your mother is wanting to marry some man in Memphis, and we haven't quite decided where you're gone live. But if you go back to Memphis, you tell her I'll not let her marry that man."

"Yessir."

Aunt Lou lived on the west side of Blytheville, where the people coming from low water areas had crowded in. Even here, there was water standing a foot deep in some places because of poor drainage. She met us at the door, fat and full of love, and hugged me hard. Daddy said, "I have you another little refugee." She just hugged me again; it was the first time I'd been hugged right in about two months.

In the living room, I saw seven or eight children all under twelve. I knew three of them. Aunt Marie, Aunt Lou's daughter who was really my cousin, came out of another room. She didn't hug me because she wasn't a hugger, but she was nice. She had never had time to marry, having devoted her life to taking care of stray kids left by various families in the Allen clan.

"Think we can find room for Alvin Junior?" Aunt Lou asked her.

"We'll find room," she said, smiling down at me. She took me back and opened a door to a little room under the staircase. It was a closet with a cot in it and a light drop hanging from the ceiling. "This will be your sleeping place until we can find you something better," she said. It turned out to be my bedroom for as long as I was there. It was comfortable enough, but when the door was closed and the light was out, it was pitch dark. It was even darker than the bedroom at Mrs. Pet's.

At least there were people to talk to here. Many of the kids were relatives, but there were others Aunt Marie had taken in because she couldn't say no to an orphan. The rain went on, so we couldn't play outside. It was crowded, but all the kids were well-mannered and didn't cause any commotion. We'd sit in the enormous living room and listen to scratchy church hymns on the big Victrola and play games all day. It never occurred to me to ask why we didn't go to school.

It was only two and a half weeks before Christmas now, and we were regimented into patterns of eating. The men ate first, then the women, and the kids last. Food wasn't plentiful, and I'm sure it was tough to come up with enough for everyone. No one complained. There were always smiles from Aunt Marie and hugs from Aunt Lou.

On Christmas Day, Aunt Marie had placed a present under the tree for every child. We had lots of devotions, and Aunt Marie talked about the Christ Child and the meaning of Christmas. My present was a pair of red suspenders.

After Christmas, we went on in the same way: we stayed in and ate our small portions of food while it rained. Then one day well into January, Aunt Marie drove up, rushed in, and told me to get my things—I was going back to Memphis on a bus they thought might get through and it was leaving in an hour. She rushed me downtown and crushed me into a Greyhound bus loaded with people going to Memphis.

The trip took all day because the driver had to stop often and wait for the water to go down. Sometimes when the bus plowed through deep water, I could hear the driver praying the motor wouldn't drown out. The highway wasn't even visible, and it seemed we were driving on top of the water.

Just after sundown, we crossed the Harahan Bridge into Memphis. When I got out at the station, I counted my thirty-five cents and decided I could spend seven cents for the Madison Avenue streetcar so I wouldn't have to walk with my suitcase and box.

My mother was beside herself when I got home. She was so moved by my arrival that all she could do was cry and tell me over and over how worried she'd been and how sorry she was about it all. She fixed a big supper and let me have two desserts.

The next day was Saturday, but my mother had to work all day at the furrier—January was a busy month for them. I checked out two dozen fresh pies from Leonard's Bakery and went to sell them to the workers at the feed mills over on the railroad. By two o'clock, I had sold all my pies and made forty cents, so I went downtown by myself to Loew's Palace Theater to see the new Tarzan moving-picture show. Afterward, I got some Krystal hamburgers and decided to walk back home down Union Avenue. It was only about two miles, and it had not rained much since I had been home. It was clear and cold, and everyone I met was talking about the water's receding and that maybe the worst of the flood was over.

Union Avenue had street lights, one after another down its length, and neon signs flashing and flickering. As I walked along, I thought about my time with Mrs. Pet in Cooter and about the little cot in the closet in Blytheville and about all that silence and darkness. It was that night I decided I really did like lights, especially in the winter. And it occurred to me that many people had been saved from the flood, but in my case, the flood had saved me from too much darkness.

8

Doodlelums

THE AUGUST I WAS eleven, I was spending the final days of
my summer vacation in the Bootheel at my Grandmother
Bradie's waiting for my mother to come from Memphis or my
daddy to come from Caruthersville to pick me up. That's the
way it always was: I never knew who was coming, but I never
worried about how I would get home. Both my parents knew
when school started, and one of them would always show up
to get me back to Memphis in time.

After working most of the summer in the relative silence that
I loved on the farm at Aunt Annie and Uncle Will's, I was usually
ready to change gears and would go to Grandmother's house
because I knew there would be more action and more kids there
among my mother's people.

One afternoon, a truck drove up in Grandmother's yard,
and I ran out expecting to see Daddy but was surprised to find
it was Aunt Mary and Uncle Otis. I knew they didn't have a truck
and probably would never be able to afford one. They'd hired
their neighbor to carry them to visit Uncle Otis's sick sister out
from Blytheville, Arkansas. Their two small children had stayed
with the neighbor's wife for the day, but Dewey was with them.

Dewey was a grown man who had lived with Aunt Mary
and Uncle Otis ever since they had gotten married, and he was
one of those things I had never figured out. He looked sort of

old but acted sort of young. He could talk but seldom did—he just sat and smiled and nodded a lot. He ate well and was a good work hand. I remember asking Aunt Annie about Dewey one time, and she said, "Well, Alvin Junior, honey, Dewey—bless his heart—is just not all there." She paused. "He's just not quite right." I could tell *this* didn't quite sound right to Aunt Annie. "The Lord takes care of Dewey," she quickly said.

Dewey came up to the front porch with Uncle Otis and Aunt Mary, and we sat and talked about crops and canning and children. There were a few vague comments about Uncle Otis's sister's illness. I wondered a little about it, but I had learned not to ask what was wrong with older women. When they'd visited enough, Aunt Mary, who looked a lot like my mother even though she was only her half sister, suggested I go home with them and wait for my ride back to Memphis there. Grandmother said that would be all right, so in a matter of minutes I had packed my little suitcase and box and was in the back of the truck with Uncle Otis and Dewey, headed to their place somewhere out from Deering.

It was so windy and noisy in the back that we couldn't talk much, but I did ask Uncle Otis about Ol' Buck, their dog, and he said Buck was doing good. We got to their tenant-farm house about dark, and Ol' Buck romped and yelped and licked me in the face till Aunt Mary said, "I'll declare, that dog cares more for you, Alvin Junior, than he does for all of us put together."

We ate supper in the kitchen by the light of two ornate kerosene lamps. (Aunt Annie always had just one on her dining table.) Afterwards I went out in the dark and played with Ol' Buck some more. Then we all went to bed.

The next day was a plain Bootheel farm day. Uncle Otis and Dewey patched up an old shed in the back. It was the time of year just before cotton picking when the days were spent mending and getting things ready for fall and winter and visiting sick relatives. Ol' Buck and I went down the road to visit the neighbor boy, Cranston, whose daddy had a huge back-house full of tools, saws, hammers, nails, and all kinds of spare lumber. I had visited up there before, and every time, we'd saw and hammer and nail and build things. We never made anything special; we'd just build things. The fun was in sawing and hammering and putting wood together. I figured Cranston was a year or two older than me. He didn't seem to know much, but he really could make things out of wood. We worked together for three days.

On Saturday morning, one of Uncle Otis's friends walked up in the yard and said he knew how he could get a ride into Caruthersville and talked Uncle Otis into going with him. I could tell Aunt Mary wasn't happy with this. After they had gone down the road and out of sight, she commented to me that his friend was a drinking man and was always getting into trouble. I stayed around the house that day, helping with the chores and playing with the two little boys, who were about three and five years old.

Toward the middle of the afternoon, Dewey sat down on the end of the porch and seemed to be watching the birds on a telephone line. Dewey was always looking at something. It was one of those hot late August days, very quiet and still and empty. I thought to myself, "I sure wish my mother or my daddy one would come and get me." I had had a wonderful summer, but I was ready for Memphis and a cool picture show.

Uncle Otis hadn't come home by the time I went to bed, and I heard Aunt Mary pacing the front room floor late into the night. At breakfast, we sat and ate in silence, and then we all went out and sat on the front porch. Later, we could hear the church bells ringing off in the distance.

"We should all be in church," Aunt Mary said.

I didn't say anything and, of course, neither did Dewey. The children seemed untroubled and hadn't even asked for their daddy.

Sunday was still very hot and even slower and quieter than Saturday had been. I tried playing with Ol' Buck, but even he was lazy. About four o'clock that afternoon, a lady came down the road from Cranston's house, called Aunt Mary out, and walked with her over to the end of the porch by the flowering vines. She talked to Aunt Mary in a low voice, so I went around to the back yard with Ol' Buck and forced him to play fetch-a-stick. He reluctantly did it about three times, and then I moseyed back around to the front yard and saw the lady walking up the road. Aunt Mary sat down in her rocker and looked straight ahead, tears running down her face.

After a while she said, "Otis is in jail again, Alvin Jr." She didn't say anything for a long time. "He and Homer Smith got into a drunken brawl, and they're both in the Caruthersville jail," she said.

"What are you gonna do, Aunt Mary?"

"I don't rightly know," she said, and she rocked a while. Finally, she told me she was going to go over to talk with Mr. Rushing, the landowner, to see if he might help.

I kept the children on Monday while Aunt Mary walked the two miles to see Mr. Rushing. Dewey took an ax and started splitting wood out back. I wondered why, since there was more than enough piled up for cooking. I played games with the children and went and fed the chickens, which wasn't much of a chore because they only had six. They didn't have a cow or hogs or any stock.

Just after noon, Aunt Mary returned looking a little downcast. Mr. Rushing had called the sheriff and found out Uncle Otis had a fifty-dollar fine. He told Aunt Mary he would not pay Otis's fine again. This was the third time Uncle Otis had been put in jail for drinking and fighting, and Mr. Rushing had bailed him out "once and no more." Uncle Otis had stayed in jail fifteen days one time the year before.

I spent the rest of that quiet Monday hoping for someone to come and get me. Late in the afternoon, a very long red truck stopped out on the road. The driver stayed behind the wheel while another man, wearing brown leather high boots, riding pants, a white shirt, and a short brown straw hat, got out and came up to the house. He introduced himself to Aunt Mary as A.J. Boyd and said he was representing a farm company in Arkansas. "I want to talk to you about Otis," the man said. He sounded real proper.

Aunt Mary seemed reluctant to tell him that Otis was in jail, so Mr. Boyd said, "I know Otis is in the Caruthersville jail, and I also know that you probably don't have the money to get him out. I'm here to try and help you." Aunt Mary's eyes lit up a little. "I will pay Otis's fine," Mr, Boyd said, "and set this whole family up in a new home with a fine farm company in Arkansas."

Aunt Mary said she wanted Otis out of jail, but she really didn't want to move. "We've moved so much," she said.

Mr. Boyd didn't seem to have paid any attention to her. He kept right on telling her all the good things about his offer, including doctor's care. Then he asked her about the size of the family and about me and Dewey. We'd been sitting at the other end of the porch but close enough that we had heard everything—at least I had.

Aunt Mary explained that I was her sister's boy waiting to go back to Memphis, and that Dewey was a very good farm hand, and that she and Uncle Otis were strong workers.

After a lot more talking, Aunt Mary agreed to take Mr. Boyd's offer. He gave her a paper to sign and said, "I'll be back with Otis to get you all in about three or four hours."

"So soon?" Aunt Mary asked, sort of shocked.

"Start packing right now and be ready to go," he said as he turned and went back to the truck. The driver started the engine, and as soon as Mr. Boyd closed his door, they shot down the road, slinging loose rocks and stirring up a choking cloud of dust.

Dewey and I went inside with Aunt Mary and helped her pack and sack things. It didn't take as long as I had thought it would; they didn't have very much. When we finished, I went down to Cranston's house before dark and asked his family to watch out for my parents and to tell whichever one they saw that Aunt Mary and Uncle Otis were being moved to Arkansas. "Best I could tell, they are moving to a farm out from Osceola, Arkansas, which is on Highway 61," I told them. "I'll send Mother and Daddy both post cards when I find out exactly where it is."

About ten o'clock that night, the long red truck returned. Uncle Otis sheepishly came into the front room where we sat waiting with Aunt Mary. They didn't hug or anything. "I guess we better get our stuff on the truck," he said. So we all pitched in and started carrying things out. As I got close to the truck bed, I could make out that it was already almost full of furniture, boxes, and suitcases. There were six or seven people sitting or lying in and around the furniture; they didn't move as we hung lanterns on the end of the truck and piled our stuff on. In less than an hour, we were all on the truck going south on Highway 61 through territory familiar to me at first. Sometime past midnight, we even passed through Steele, where I was born.

I found a place on a mattress with Ol' Buck and kept close watch on my suitcase and box. Though it was still August and it had been very warm as we loaded, the wind whipped through the open truck, and I started to get cold. I huddled up with Ol' Buck to keep warm. Dewey seemed to be watching the stars. It was a clear, moonless night, and there were an awful lot of stars. I remembered what Aunt Annie had told me about God's promise to Abraham in the Old Testament. "His descendants would be as numerous as the stars in the sky," she had said. I tried to count them for a while and wondered why I had never seen a Jew.

Somewhere out from Blytheville, Arkansas, the truck stopped on the side of the road, and the driver yelled back, "It's time for a stop. Men on the right side of the road, women on the left." I had relieved myself outdoors before when no privy was available, but never this close to a road and to other people. I was suddenly very lonesome relieving myself there in the dark with everyone else. We got back in the truck and I slept a while.

Somewhere past Osceola, the truck turned west on a gravel road, and after another half hour and several turns, we stopped. The driver got out on the running board and yelled back, "It'll be daylight in about an hour; we'll wait and unload then." I climbed up on the side gate and saw Mr. Boyd disappear down the road in the darkness. I never went back to sleep.

As daylight came, everyone was curious to see where we were and what things looked like. It got light pretty fast as sort of a hazy fog cleared with sunup. The gravel road we were on ran north and south. There were five houses on the west side of the road and five on the east side. They all looked brand new, had green tin roofs, and were painted yellow.

Behind the east houses, cotton was everywhere as far as I could see. A thick woods began about two hundred yards behind the west houses and ran as far as I could see to the north and south. It was full of gigantic cypress trees and water oaks, and I figured it had just recently been drained. I wondered if it were even thick enough to be called a forest. There were stumps and piles of logs around the west houses, and to the south, between the road and the woods, was a huge barn. Beyond that a quarter of a mile was a big white house. It was pretty clear to me after looking around that the part of the farm I could see was newly cleared land and that the wooded west side was soon to be.

The driver came back and told us to unload, and I thought it odd that the other people on the truck, who had paid us no attention throughout the night before, all pitched in and helped move Uncle Otis and Aunt Mary's furniture and stuff off first. By two hours after sunup, we had everything in the very first house on the west side. It was the house farthest south and the one closest to the big barn. Then we all helped the two other families move into their houses down the road.

Around noon, some people already living there wandered down and made acquaintance with Uncle Otis. They were not overly friendly, but one older woman brought down a skillet of cornbread and some rabbit stew. Aunt Mary divided it up on plates, and it was gone fast.

After dinner, Dewey helped Uncle Otis put up stoves in the living room and kitchen. Like most houses in those days, there were four rooms: two bedrooms, a front room, and a large kitchen for cooking and eating. I guess the yellow and green paint was an attempt to make those raw houses look a little cheerful. One thing I noticed right off was that the mosquitoes were pretty bad even during the day.

By the middle of the afternoon, just about everything had been squared away, but we were all too addled to be at ease. It had been a long day, and I wondered what else would happen before bedtime. Even Ol' Buck seemed a little disturbed with all the confusion and newness. Dewey stood in the back yard and looked at the big, thick woods.

Before dusk, Mr. Boyd came riding down from the big white house on a fine black horse. He rode into the yard and, without getting down, asked Uncle Otis how things were going. "As good as you would expect," Uncle Otis said.

"We'll all get to work tomorrow," Mr. Boyd said. "Lots to do here before cotton picking." He turned his horse and checked in at several other houses before he went back up the road to the big white house.

The next day, Uncle Otis and Dewey went down the road a piece with the other men to work at clearing the woods. About mid-morning, Mr. Boyd rode by and saw me playing with Ol' Buck in the yard. He stopped and told me I should go over to the big barn and help shuck corn. "Everyone works around here," he said.

I took Ol' Buck to the barn. There in the middle of the floor was a huge pile of corn and several women and children shucking. I had shucked a lot of corn in my life, so I jumped in and got a quite a bit done before dinner. One thing I didn't like was the big mice running around in and out of the corn. No one seemed to be afraid of them, so I didn't show my concern. They must have been shucking for several days, because there were several cribs full of shucked corn and a mound about fifteen feet high over to the side.

That night, two men came down to see Uncle Otis. While they sat and talked, I listened. From what I heard, none of them had been there very long, and all had been sort of tricked one way or another into moving there. They complained about being paid off with doodlelums.

"What do you mean, you're paid off with doodlelums?" Uncle Otis asked.

"Well," the older man said, "Mr. Boyd and his paymaster meet in front of the barn at noon on Saturday, and they give each family a book of doodlelums. You get no money. And you get your groceries and goods at the Myrtle store with them dood-lelums."

"Where's the Myrtle store?" Uncle Otis asked.

"It's the company store about seven miles from here. There'll be a truck to carry you in at two o'clock on Saturday, and it comes back at five o'clock."

The older man had done most of the talking. Finally the younger man said, "You know you can't leave this place, don't you?"

Uncle Otis looked sort of surprised.

"You came here in debt, and your debt gets more and more, and they won't let you leave till you settle up," the younger man explained. "Too, you can see the doctor on Saturday, but they charge you big, and it makes your debt bigger and bigger."

"Some folks don't think it's all that bad," the older man said. "At least everyone eats."

They talked on an hour or so, and the older man told a story about a man who worked for the same farm company some three miles away. He was deep in debt to the company with no hope of ever getting out, but somehow he hired a man out of Luxora to come with a wagon and mules to carry him and his family and all of his belongings out of there. The man had stood up in the middle of the wagon with his wife and children huddled around him. When they got to the company farm border, there were men there with guns and a sheriff, but he went right on by and there was no shooting.

"I've heard that story, too," the younger man said, "but I've also heard of people getting shot, and I heard of a whole family that just disappeared."

They sat a while.

"I came here last spring and owed the company a hundred and sixty dollars," the younger man said. "I asked them last month about my debt, and they said now I owe 'em three hundred."

"It's them doodlelums," the older man said. "You never know what they're worth."

They talked on into the night.

The men worked till suppertime again on Thursday, but on Friday, Mr. Boyd let them come home early in the afternoon to get ready for cotton picking on Monday. Uncle Otis had been making rabbit box traps at night, so he finished up a third one before supper and asked me to help him carry them into the woods. I had long since decided Aunt Mary and Uncle Otis had moved to a terrible place, but there was something wonderful about those woods. In the woods, the smell was so clean, and there was still lots of green, and little streams of water moved in and out around the trees. We walked pretty far back in before we set out the three traps, which were nothing but long wooden boxes—each with a trap door on one end that would fall down once a rabbit triggered a baited stick inside. "We'll check 'em out tomorrow," he said.

As we crossed the little streams on the way back to the house, Uncle Otis would stop and look at all the animal tracks in the mud on the banks. He was pretty smart about that sort of thing. He made some comments about there being lots of bobcats in the woods, and I noticed that the mosquitoes were even worse back in there. When it started to grow dark, I became more and more aware of sounds I had never heard before, and I was relieved to get back to the little yellow and green house and the kerosene glow of Aunt Mary's ornate lamps.

All through these days, I watched for a car that might be Daddy or Mother coming to get me. I was ready to go.

On Saturday after dinner, everyone gathered at the big barn, and Mr. Boyd and the paymaster both rode down on fine black horses. Mr. Boyd called out names and handed out little books of doodlelums. Uncle Otis got his book, and we went back to the house to prepare for the truck ride into Myrtle for supplies. He let me look at his books; they had different colored tickets with 5, 10, 25, and on up to 100 printed on them—kind of like play money. I asked if I could go in to Myrtle with him, and he said, "Sure, if you want to."

We got on the truck with about fifteen other men. They were different ages, but all of them had weathered and solemn-looking faces. As we drove the seven miles into Myrtle, we passed at least five or six other little rows of houses similar to ours. All of them were painted bright colors. I remember thinking that it certainly was a big farm company. Then I thought about all those solemn people that lived behind the cheerful paint of those pitiful little houses and was reminded of one of Aunt Annie's Bible readings about "whited sepulchres" that were whitewashed to look nice on the outside, but on the inside they were full of dead men's bones.

At Myrtle, the store was full of people looking over food, overalls, tobacco, and all kinds of supplies. Myrtle was nothing but that one store, a cotton gin, and a small house used by the doctor on Saturdays. There were about ten people waiting in line at the doctor's door.

I had two dollars hidden in my pockets. (My *big* money—the total of my summer savings from carrying water at Uncle Will's—I had converted to three ten-dollar bills and stuffed up inside a loose sole of one of an old pair of shoes that I kept in my little suitcase. I had learned not to have any money around my mother's people. It wasn't that they stole; it's just that they usually needed money and had been known to ask for loans and never pay them back.) I quickly found the important stuff in the store and got me a Pepsi, a Powerhouse candy bar, a sack of peanut brittle, and two penny postcards. I walked up to the counter and put down a real dollar bill. Several people looked at me strange. The man behind the counter sort of acted as if I was doing something wrong, but he gave me my change and I went outside.

I took out a pencil I had remembered to bring and wrote my mother and my daddy both desperate messages on the postcards and tried to give them specific directions to where I was. Then I went back inside the store and dropped them in a slot for mail. For a while, I just sat and finished drinking my Pepsi and watched people until Uncle Otis came to the door with two towsacks full of groceries. He said he didn't have enough doodlelums, but they put the difference on the books.

At five o'clock, we got on the truck with everyone else and headed back to the houses by the edge of the woods as the day grew gray and then dark.

Early Sunday morning, I followed Uncle Otis back into the woods to the rabbit traps. All three doors were down, and Uncle Otis pulled two gray-brown rabbits from the first two boxes. For some unexplainable reason, there was no rabbit in the third box—the bait was gone, too. Uncle Otis didn't make much of the mystery. He just took the other rabbits one at a time, held them by their hind legs, and whacked them with the side of his hand across the backs of their necks. They didn't even jerk. "I've never seen that," I said, trying not to sound shocked. Uncle Otis was good at such things. He rebaited the traps, and we returned to the house, where he cleaned and dressed the rabbits.

I realized it was Sunday and I had not seen a church of any kind on the entire company farm. Then I thought that even if they did have a church, those folks would have nothing but doodlelums to put in the collection plate. This sure would make it strange for a preacher, I thought.

I kept watching the road for my folks to come and get me. The afternoon passed slowly, but I went down to the big barn and rode a mule named Sal with some of the other children. We took turns. I had seen several people riding Sal around on the farm and learned that day that she was a good and gentle mule.

Monday morning, everyone who was able and didn't have babies to take care of started picking cotton at sunup. I didn't, and no one told me I had to. Word had gotten around that I was a city boy and my daddy had money. Too, in just those few days, Uncle Otis had told everybody that John Barnes Thompson back in Missouri was my uncle. Everyone, even those crooked farm company bosses, knew of Mr. Thompson's reputation as the meanest, toughest, richest landowner in the Missouri Bootheel, which was a part of the country known for mean, tough characters. Anyway, I let them believe it about my daddy having money. Sometimes he had money; sometimes he didn't. And I didn't volunteer any information about my relationship with Mr. Thompson. Uncle Otis had also told everyone that someone would be coming to get me any day.

After breakfast, Aunt Mary said Uncle Otis had left word for me to check the rabbit traps. She also said she hoped the traps were empty, because she did not believe in eating rabbits until after the first frost. I got Ol' Buck, took a towsack, and started back into the woods. There seemed to be more birds in the trees than ever that day, and again there was that wonderful smell found only in the deep woods. I always felt good back in there.

When I got to the traps, there was only one door down, so I carefully eased my hand in to get the rabbit by the legs. When I got it out, it dawned on me that Uncle Otis wasn't there to kill it. It was such a sweet little rabbit. I thought about it a long time; then I half-heartedly tried to whack its neck, but it only squealed a little. So I put it in the sack and returned with it jumping around.

As I walked into the back yard, Aunt Mary saw the sack jumping around and said, "Turn it loose, Alvin Junior. Turn it loose." I was so glad. I opened the sack and watched the rabbit bound back into the woods. That night, we told Uncle Otis the truth about the rabbit, and he just shook his head in disgust.

It was now one week into September and I knew school had already started in Memphis. I kept watching the road, but there were other things to watch, too. One day while the younger children were riding Sal near the barn, a brown hound dog came chasing a bobcat out of a thicket on the edge of the woods. In a field near the barn, the bobcat suddenly turned and grabbed the hound by the nose with his mouth. I'd never heard a dog yelp so loud. The bobcat held on for a long, long time as they rolled and flopped. Finally the bobcat let go and ran into the woods. Blood was all over the dog's face as it too ran off into the woods in a different direction, still yelping in pain. That's the day I added bobcats to my list of serious fears, that up till then had included only mad dogs and blue racer snakes. That hound dog never came out of the woods.

At night, everyone talked about how much cotton they'd picked. Dewey seemed excited about picking three hundred pounds on the very first day. However, I heard the men talking about how fertile the land was in that newly cleared section, which caused the cotton to be long and heavy. One day, just for fun, I went to the fields and saw that the cotton was higher than my head. I had picked cotton in the Bootheel and thought it might be fun to see how much I could pick here—but since they had decided I was someone important, I decided to stay out of it.

About midweek, Dewey got real sick with a fever, and Aunt Mary was half sick. Then Uncle Otis got the sickness. That Thursday morning, all three grownups were in bed with fever and weren't able to go to the fields to pick cotton. Some lady from down the road who knew a lot about sicknesses visited, looked at them, and said, "Well, it looks like you've got malaria, but it might be rabbit fever or pump water fever." She gave Uncle Otis an empty bottle of some medicine that could be bought over at a store off the company farm at Kimball about five miles to the northeast. "Of course, you have to have real money because it's across the company line," she said.

The next day they were worse. About noon, Uncle Otis said weakly, "Alvin Junior, you've got to go try to get us some of that medicine." I expressed some concern about walking because of mad dogs, blue racers snakes, and bobcats. "You can ride that mule Sal," he said. "You can do it." Then he sent me down two houses to talk to a man in charge of the barn.

I came back to tell Uncle Otis it was okay to borrow Sal, and he asked me if I had any money. I told him I had a dollar and forty-two cents in my pocket, which was true. Then he and Aunt Mary scrounged around and found pennies and nickels left over from the Bootheel days until they had about three dollars. I put all the money and the empty medicine bottle in a little sack, put on my straw hat, and started out toward Kimball on Sal a little after one o'clock. I had been instructed by the man in charge of the barn to go due north for two-and-a-half miles and then turn right and go straight for another two-and-a-half miles. There I would find Kimball. He said I would know where to turn because the gravel would stop and I would turn onto a dirt road.

Sal was a very slow mule, but we got along with no problems for maybe a mile. Then for no reason at all except that she was a mule, Sal just stopped. I said, "Giddyap, Sal," but she wouldn't move. After I had hit her rump with my hand several times and she still didn't move, I began to wonder if Sal could see something that I couldn't, like Balaam's donkey who saw an angel of the Lord holding a sword and blocking the road. Maybe God was preventing Sal from taking me somewhere I shouldn't go. I tried hard to remember my scriptures, and I recalled that Balaam kept beating till that donkey finally turned around and talked to him. So I figured the best way to determine God's will would be to just keep slapping Sal's rump till she talked or walked. Finally, after about six more giddyaps and a lot of slapping, she started to move again.

I did not pass a single house in that first two-and-a-half miles. The thick woods had continued on the west side of the road and the clear fields on the east side, but up here, most of the fields were in hay or corn instead of cotton. Sal stopped again before I got to the turnoff and three more times on the dirt road after the turn. It was way past the middle of the afternoon when I could see the little town not far away.

Just before I got to the edge of town, I saw a man with a shotgun walking out from a small house to the road. When we passed, I spoke to him, but he just nodded his head a little and said nothing.

Kimball was a town of about four store-looking buildings, but I could see some nice houses on down a bit. There was one two-story building that looked more important than the others, so I tied Sal up to a post and went inside. It was the right place. I walked past three old men sitting on a bench and on to the back, where I was greeted by a real nice man, who looked like he might be the owner. I told him about the sick folks and showed him the empty medicine bottle.

"How many capsules do you want?" he asked. He sounded smart.

I poured all the money that was in the sack on the counter and said, "As many as I can get with what's left after I buy me a Pepsi and a Milky Way candy bar."

He pushed a dime to the side, counted the rest, reached inside a glass display cabinet, and placed a candy bar on the counter. "You get your Pepsi in the cold drink box up front," he said. "I'll get your capsules."

I sat down and really guzzled that Pepsi long before I started eating the Milky Way. The old men just looked at me. As soon as the druggist brought me the capsules, I put them in my pocket, went out, untied old Sal, and started back. I saw a horse trough with a pump by a closed-down blacksmith shop, so I primed the pump with a bucket of water and pumped Sal some water in the trough. I didn't think she would ever quit drinking.

I finally pulled her away from the trough, climbed on, and we started back. When we got to the edge of town, the man with the gun stayed on the house porch. I could tell Sal knew she was going home because her gait was a little faster. It was then I first estimated that we didn't have enough daylight to get back before dark. I got a little nervous. It wasn't that I was so afraid of the *dark,* but in the dark a body can't tell that things are sneaking up from behind—things like bobcats.

By the time we turned the corner with still two-and-a-half miles to go, the sun was down and the sky was gray. I slapped Sal on her rump, but she had only two speeds: slow and slower. I had to settle for slow. Darkness fell with about a mile still to go, and all the night sounds began. I could hear things rustling in the weeds on the sides of the road, and I started worrying about whether mules could see in the dark. For years I'd bragged at school in Memphis about my country adventures, but I promised myself that, if I got through this ordeal, I'd never brag again. It seemed forever, but at last I could see faint lights from distant windows, and then in a few minutes we were back to the yellow houses.

I took Sal to the big barn, took off her bridle and bit, and turned her loose. I took the capsules into the house and started acting like a doctor. I pumped fresh, cool water for Aunt Mary, Uncle Otis, and Dewey to drink, and I put cool rags on their sick heads. Someone had brought over some soup and biscuits. The soup was cold now, but I helped them eat a little and fed the children. All three grownups were really sick. Uncle Otis and Aunt Mary groaned and moaned, but Dewey took his sickness well and never groaned at all.

After a while, I went out to sit on the porch and hugged Ol' Buck. "Ol' Buck, this is a funny world," I said, and he didn't disagree.

Uncle Otis and Dewey were still very ill on Friday, but Aunt Mary managed to get around and help nurse the men and cook a little. Saturday, all three were better, but Uncle Otis was disappointed that he was still too sick and weak to go on a big coon hunt scheduled for Saturday night. After I went to bed, I heard the yelping dogs and the guns shooting all night out in the woods. The next morning there was a pile of more than thirty coons in the back yard two houses down, and two men were cleaning and dressing them. The people next door were given all the coon livers, so they invited us to a coon liver dinner since we had had so much sickness. Thank goodness they had good gravy.

I didn't let on, but I really didn't care much for coon livers and ate as few as I could and still be polite.

Sunday night I sat on the front porch and talked to Ol' Buck some more.

About midday on Monday, I saw a shiny new car coming up the road from the south. It was Daddy. Everyone but Aunt Mary and the children were out in the fields picking cotton. I hugged Aunt Mary, the children, and Ol' Buck goodbye, got my suitcase and box, and was soon leaving the company farm in style with my Daddy. When we reached Highway 61, there was a big, beautiful white mansion sitting back in the trees. Daddy said that was where the owners of the company farm lived. "They don't treat their farm hands very fair around here," he said. "Your Uncle Otis is in a bad place."

"Yes," I said, "I figured that out right away."

We rode a little way in silence as I waited for him to explain why it took him so long to come for me. He didn't volunteer any information, and I wanted to ask him. Before I could get my words together, Daddy said, "You should not have gone off with them. For the life of me, I don't see what you see in your mother's people." I sat quietly for a while. Then he said, "Do you have any of your money left?" His tone was friendlier.

"Yessir. It's stuffed in my shoe in my suitcase."

He smiled and said, "Smart boy."

Back in Memphis, the school principal made me sit one full day on the punishment bench outside his office for being two weeks late for the opening of school. It wasn't as embarrassing as it might have been, because all the children knew that I had been adventuring in the country.

Late the next spring, my Grandpa Pete was brought to Memphis from the Bootheel for special treatment of a black widow spider bite on his leg. I could hardly stand to look at it, it was so swollen and black and blue.

One night while he was recuperating at the little house where Mother and I lived, he told me the story of how Uncle T.L. and Uncle Charlie took all the money they had to hire a man over in Kennett, Missouri, to drive his small truck down the back roads in the middle of the night to the big company farm and steal Aunt Mary, Uncle Otis, Dewey, and the children out of Arkansas. "They had to leave all their furniture." Grandpa Pete hesitated for a while before adding, "And they also had to leave Ol' Buck behind." He looked at me a for a little bit and said, "There just wasn't room. Otis said Ol' Buck chased after the truck for a long time in the darkness until they couldn't see him any more."

I didn't let Grandpa Pete see how I felt. I went out in the backyard and cried.

9

—

Earlus

MOST RESPECTABLE MOTHERS IN our neighborhood of Memphis told their young sons to steer clear of Earlus Johnson. My mother was very respectable, so I kept my unusual friendship with Earlus a secret. In fact, hardly anyone knew about our association, which was really a business partnership, because none of Earlus's friends liked me and none of my friends liked him.

I understood why Mother didn't want me to run around with Earlus; he was considered a very tough boy from a very tough family in a very tough neighborhood. His father had disappeared not long after the last of the houseful of kids was born. After that, his mother spent a year in prison for trying to feed her family through some illegal means, and all the kids were hauled off to Saint Peter's Orphanage. I remember walking by the orphanage one time and talking to Earlus through the big iron fence—I think I was in the third grade. It seems I'd known him for a long time then; I don't know when or how I first met him.

I had heard that Earlus always carried knives and was famous for throwing them and that he would steal anything, but my dealings with him, starting in about the fourth grade, were always in honest business schemes. He never displayed any of these undesirable traits in my company. We gathered and sold kindling sticks for five cents a bundle. On some Saturday mornings, we'd sell fresh pies from Leonard's Bakery to the men in the feed mills, clearing twenty cents a dozen. We'd push rainflooded cars for whatever we could get.

My mother never asked questions when I'd tell her I was going out to try to make some money. During the Depression, that was an acceptable endeavor, and she trusted me to do right. She had taught me to take care of myself and to refuse offers of cigarettes and other bad things that I'd encounter in the city. I don't think Mother knew about The Skillet and Buzz Brady and their gangs of thugs who patrolled the streets looking for younger boys, whom they scared into paying protection money or else beat to a pulp. But she did know that I'd be home at a decent hour and usually with some legitimate earnings. I never told her that most of my profits were the product of Earlus's brain and brawn.

When I was in the fifth grade, Earlus approached me with an enterprising money-making idea. He knew where pigeons nested in the nooks and crannies of old housetops around town and had learned that we could sell squabs for fifty cents a pair at the Hotel Peabody, which was famous for its squab sandwiches and other delicacies. He needed me for a cover man—someone to hide, watch, and whistle up a warning if a householder or policeman got suspicious while he was rambling around in the eaves. Sometimes he'd have to drop the smelly babies from a precarious perch, and I'd have to make a straw landing nest for them. It was also my job to find a box in which to haul our mess each time we went out. We always tried to find at least four pairs so that we'd get a dollar each for our work.

I often wondered why Earlus picked me for this secret mission. I guess it was because I was pretty much of a solo type and all his other friends ran in twos and threes or more. I had long ago decided to believe that he wasn't as bad as his reputation, and I soon learned from our squab business that he was the bravest person I had ever known.

Earlus was about the same height and, I guess, the same age as I was, but he was hard-twisted, very street-wise, and seemed a lot older. He was usually dirty—my Mother said he was rusty one time when she saw him—and it was hard to tell what color his hair was. He could climb to the top of anything. I remember watching him one Saturday from my lookout spot on the ground as he crawled like a spider up a drainage pipe on the corner of an old red house that seemed unusually tall. As he neared the roof, the pipe tore loose and leaned out with Earlus hanging on to its tip. I was frozen with fear as he dangled there for an instant like a tattered flag. Suddenly he made a dramatic leap and caught hold of the gutter along the edge of the roof and walked hand-over-hand until he got to an angle where he could more easily make his way up to the chimney. He never looked afraid or even startled. He looked almost disinterested, as if death were just another possibility he faced every day, and if he should fall and die, that was just the way it was.

I never showed him how fearful I was for him or how scared I was when we'd get caught in the act. Yes, there were times when we got caught, but we never got grabbed—no one was fast enough for that. There were also times when people thought they had caught us in the act, but while they were peering up at the roof, I'd whistle up a warning, and in three minutes Earlus could be seen walking innocently up the street from at least three houses down. Then we'd both stand and look with the rest of the curious neighbors. Of course it never occurred to us to stop and explain that we were merely trying to earn some honest dollars by cleaning pesky birds out of their rooftops. Then again, it wasn't safe for dirty little boys who looked very much like prowlers to stop and explain.

Sometimes I'd climb up with Earlus when we thought there'd be more squabs than could be stuffed into one shirt and it was too risky to make two trips from the nests to the edge of the roof to drop them. There were times when we waded through old attics ankle deep with pigeon manure to make a big haul. There were also times when I couldn't climb all the way. Earlus always seemed pleased with this sign of his superiority, but he never called me chicken. He'd just grin and say, "Okay, Alvin, you stay right there," as he shinnied up to greater heights. He must have been on top of every house in Memphis to know as much as he did about the squab crop. He was uncanny in his timing, too. They had to be harvested one week to ten days before their mothers pushed them out of their nests. Before then they were too small, and after, they would fly the nest.

It was a filthy job, and even Earlus realized that we might not be welcome at the restaurant door without first washing off the worst of what we'd been through. So it was our custom to stop at one of the many purifying stations of the City Water Works before we got to Hotel Peabody. We'd scale over the high wire fence, where we'd hang our polluted clothes, and run wildly through the shallow water among the thousands of sprayers. When we'd finished our cleansing rite, we'd put our dirty clothes back on, pick up our box of smelly, mite-infested squabs, and head for the Peabody.

We kept up this business as weather permitted for about two years. I'm not sure if Earlus tried it solo during the summer months when I always went back to Missouri to work and visit with relatives, but he was always ready to go when I got back. One Saturday morning just after I'd returned from Missouri and about a week before I was to start the seventh grade, I heard Earlus whistle while I was finishing breakfast. I gulped my milk and told Mother I was going out to try to make some money. "I'll expect you back in time for supper," she called after me.

Earlus and I never wasted much time with polite talk. We hurried to hop an Elmwood streetcar and went downtown. There was always room on the back for two people to hold on to the pulleys and rest their feet on the bumpers, but we had to be careful because the police watched for hangers-on.

We rode about six blocks and got off to walk so we could check houses along the way. Earlus knew of a dozen houses where there were usually nests, and we planned to check them all. By noon, we had found only two pairs; most of the ones we found were too small, and some nests were already empty. Earlus was disappointed but by no means ready to give up. We hiked to downtown Memphis, where he knew of a dozen more good housetops. Finally we found a big old yellow house that was usually good for four or five nests, he said. I hid and watched in the hedge across the street as Earlus went up. Pretty soon I heard his signal for a good find. I snuck around to see if he needed to

Roads That Seldom Curve

drop any, but he was already on his way down the drainage pipe, his shirt bulging with four squabs.

It was almost three-thirty and we were a mile and a half from the Peabody. We didn't take time to go by the Water Works but ran and walked and ran through the back alleys to the restaurant door. We knocked on the door and stood breathlessly waiting with our stinky box of jostled, noisy babies. The man that usually bought our squabs came to the door and asked us to wait. After a few minutes, he came back and said, "For the first time I can remember, we have more squabs than we can use. I'm sorry, we just can't buy any more today." We tried to look pitiful, but he wouldn't change his line. He left us at the door, and we just sat in the alley —a dirty, tired, forlorn pair of Depression kids with a box of useless, squawky squabs.

While we sat there feeling sorry for ourselves, the Peabody man came back out and said, "Look, I really feel bad that I can't buy your birds, but I think you might be able to sell them to the kitchen at Saint Joseph Hospital. They use them there sometimes. If you go, ask for Mr. Ferguson."

Earlus brightened with new hope. We thanked the Peabody man and walked the two miles north to Saint Joseph. We poked around until we found the back door to the kitchen and knocked. Finally a big bullish-looking woman wearing a white dress and a hairnet came to the door. "What do you want?" she demanded.

"We want to talk to Mr. Ferguson," I said.

"He ain't here; come back tomorrow."

"But we have some squabs and they told us you might need some," I persisted.

"Mr. Ferguson does the buyin' and he ain't here. Come back tomorrow." She started to slam the door.

"But we live across town and we've worked all day to find these. We'll sell 'em cheap..."

"No," she yelled and slammed the door.

I picked up the cumbersome box, and we walked dejectedly for about two blocks and sat down in the shaded, stone coolness in front of a big church. As we sat there wondering what to do with our big find, a man in priestly vestments walked up. "What's wrong, boys?" he asked in a kind voice.

"We're squab hunters," I began. "We've hunted all day long to get these four pairs, but the Peabody didn't need any, and we came all the way over here to Saint Joseph's, and they told us to come back tomorrow. Now we're five miles from home, and the sun's about to go down, and we don't know what to do with these squabs."

"That's as sad a story as I've ever heard," he said. He pointed to Earlus and said, "Young man, you bring your box and come with me. I think I know how you can sell your squabs."

"Do you want me to come?" I asked.

"No, you wait for him here." He opened the tall, carved wooden doors and disappeared with Earlus.

I waited on the cathedral steps for at least half an hour, and for some reason, I started to worry. I decided to go in and look for Earlus. I could barely pull open the huge door. When I did, I peeped in and saw nothing but darkness. As my eyes adjusted to the dark, I started down a long hallway to the left. I didn't know where it led, and I was always a little afraid of the dark. When I'd gone about forty yards, I saw a doorway. I looked into a little office dimly sunlit by arched windows and saw the priest holding Earlus, whose pants were half off. Earlus had a bewildered look on his face. Both of them saw me, and for a split second, we were all stunned, I guess. I turned and ran.

Halfway down the hall, I heard Earlus yelling, "Wait for me!" His cursing and crying echoed down the long hall as I ran out the door and the church clock struck six. I ran two blocks before I looked back to see Earlus catching up with me. He was still crying as he yelled, "We can catch the six-forty." The six-forty was a Southern Line train that left the downtown terminal every evening and ran diagonally through the city. The dead end of the spur was just a few blocks away. We kept running and Earlus kept crying and yelling, "We lost our squabs! We lost our squabs!"

As we approached the dead end, the six-forty, which never had more than eight or nine cars, was just easing out. Earlus had taught me how to grab the bar, hang, swing out, and put my foot on the step. He always caught a car toward the front, but I always pretended not to be able to catch the train until the last car so I wouldn't be run over if I fell. We both jumped on the last car this time and rode to Vance Avenue. It was dusky dark as we walked the six blocks to my house. Earlus seemed to be calmed down some, but there were clean spots on his face where tears had washed off the dirt and soot.

"Alvin," he said, "you have to promise you won't ever tell anyone what happened to me today."

"I promise, Earlus."

"What was that SOB doing, anyway, Alvin? Just what was he doing?"

"I don't know, Earlus."

Neither of us had ever seen or heard of anything like what that priest was doing. What seemed even more unusual to me, though, were the tear stains on the face of a boy who could climb to any height, hop any train, go through any dark alley. He made me promise five times before I got home that I wouldn't ever tell a soul.

After school started, we went squab hunting three or four times, but we were never as successful as we had been. Our friendship wasn't the same, either. The next year, I heard that Earlus had broken into a big, fancy houseboat on the Mississippi and spent the afternoon sailing saucers and dinner plates into the river just to see them skip and sink. The police caught him—and grabbed him—when there were only three dishes left. I don't know what they did to him, but he was in trouble again a few months later. Somehow he started a laundry truck early one morning and drove down Lamar Avenue picking up fresh doughnuts that had been delivered at the doors of restaurants. When the police caught him, he had thirty-six dozen doughnuts. I decided to steer clear of Earlus, and that was the end of the squab-hunting.

When I was in the tenth grade, I heard Earlus had lied about his age to join the Air Corps. The recruiters had a pretty good pitch in the early forties, promising glamorous careers to young boys who usually ended up as vulnerable gunners in airplane bellies. The last time I saw him was when he came home to visit after training camp. He had walked by school just as it turned out. He was all clean—even his fingernails—and his hair was no longer sooty but sandy blond. Several girls had gathered around to admire his uniform as I walked up to him. "So you're really in the Air Corps," I said.

He stepped away from the girls and said, "I guess so. I figured it would keep me out of trouble, and so far it beats wading through pigeon droppings."

"Well, I hope you have good luck, Earlus," I said, extending my hand. As he took my hand, he led me a few steps farther away from the girls and asked, "Alvin, you never told anyone about that day in the church, did you?"

"No, Earlus, I've kept my promise—never told a soul."

He looked relieved and said, "I knew you wouldn't tell." Just then one of the girls called his name. He winked at me and walked back to his admirers. They looked a little young to me, but then Earlus was the expert at knowing when to clean out the nest.

10

Sophye Olive Hot Tamale Inky Stinky Fink

DURING THE SPRING OF my sixth-grade year at St. Paul Elementary School, all of my classmates began to talk about the fearful things we would encounter at Bellevue Junior High School. St. Paul was a very small public school in the central part of Memphis, and Bellevue—located about twelve blocks east of St. Paul—was one of the largest junior highs in the state. Of all the rumors, the two most horrifying were about the belt line, a gauntlet of swinging leather all seventh grade boys had to run through after the first day of school, and about the doom of getting Miss Sophye Olive Fink for a teacher.

By the end of the school year, thoughts of spending a whole summer in the Bootheel had taken my mind off these rumors. I also got a passing report card, which elated me even though I'd never been in danger of failure. At that age, I was still awed at the rite of promotion. So I went to Missouri and spent a wonderful, carefree summer.

I came back to Memphis about a week before school started so I could get ready, and the fears that were planted that spring took up a phenomenal growth rate. I spent the last night before the dreaded first day sewing some very tough but thin cardboard into the seat of the pants I planned to wear. The next morning, the day of doom, I put another pair of pants on over them in preparation for the belt line and walked stiffly to Bellevue and into the giant auditorium, where about four hundred kids had gathered to receive their homeroom assignments.

Mr. Marvel, the principal, gave us a long welcome full of rules and expectations before announcing that there would be ten sections of the seventh grade. We all knew that students would be ranked from very good to very bad by sections, but even the fear of being assigned to seven-ten with the dumbest of dummies was not as bad as the fear of getting Miss Fink for a homeroom teacher. I waited in the stuffy heat of the crowded auditorium and my double pants while Mr. Marvel called all of seven-one, seven-two, and seven-three to follow their teachers to their homerooms. The suspense and discomfort were almost unbearable.

"The following students will be in seven-four, and your homeroom teacher will be Miss Fink."

An agonized, collective groan emerged from the unfortunates whose names were yet to be called, and the next sound I heard was Mr. Marvel's voice intoning, "Alvin L. Allen."

Nothing in my young life had stunned me like that announcement. After months of dread, my worst nightmare was coming true. There she stood in her black dress. No one knew how old she was, but she was *old,* probably dodging some mandatory retirement law in her sheer determination to make life miserable for her students. She looked at least five feet ten inches tall and was built solid. Her formidable figure was covered with chalky white, sagging skin and topped with a purple wig that sat sometimes on the middle of her head, sometimes on one side, and sometimes on the other. Everyone knew she had lost all her hair years ago because of some disease. I guess the wig was originally black and had just faded into its unnatural color through the years. I had heard that it used to be blue. It didn't look anything like hair; it was just a purple thing on top of her head.

I stood up painfully and walked as slowly as I could to stand behind her as the rest of the thirty-five students in our section were called. Then we filed out and down the hall to her room on the second floor, where she took us in one at a time and showed us to our seats. Naturally, she gave me the first seat on the first row and lined up the rest of her victims in alphabetical order. The class was dead silent as she stood up front and talked on and on about thrift, honesty, cleanliness, and character. The part on cleanliness seemed strange coming from her since she had the reputation of giving off a foul odor. It was true that she didn't look very clean, but she didn't actually stink. "Of all of these attributes, the greatest is thrift," she said.

About fifteen minutes into her sermon, I heard for the first time the famous chant. Evidently a group of older students had broken out to form the chorus, and their strains wafted from the ground below our second-story window almost like theme music at a movie short: *Sophye Olive Hot Tamale Inky Stinky FINK.* They sang it several times, growing louder with each repetition, until I actually began to squirm in embarrassment for the purple-headed old lady. She never even seemed to hear them.

"Thrift builds character," she said, explaining how she had taught thrift to all of her students through the years by the method of banking, "and you will learn it in this manner also. Every Monday morning when I take roll, you will come forward when your name is called and bank a nickel. At the end of the year, you will be rewarded by seeing how much money you will have saved, and you can then use it for something worthwhile instead of frittering it away a nickel at a time as you would have had you not banked it."

She said there would also be a special treat at the end of the year for those who consistently brought their nickels every Monday. Then she described the embarrassment she would inflict upon anyone who dared come to class on a Monday without his nickel: she would announce the culprit's name and crime to the class and force him to stand at the front of the room and face the rest of the students as they came up to make their deposits.

She droned on, reinforcing everyone's fears for the full thirty-minute homeroom period. Just before the bell, the chant came again through the trees and into the window: *Sophye Olive Hot Tamale Inky Stinky FINK.* She remained oblivious and I remained horrified as we filed out. For the rest of the morning, I would dread having to come back to her room for history at one o'clock.

Somehow I survived the rest of the day. History was no worse than homeroom—and not much different, just longer. The last bell did not signal relief, because I still had to get through the belt line before I could go home. There was no way to escape this second horrible fate of the day. All seventh grade boys had heard the word that eighth- and ninth-graders would be waiting at every exit to grab them and escort them to the back, where two lines of belt-wielding boys stretched the entire length of the football field and a few yards beyond. I had been advised to run fast through the line and be careful not to fall and, above all, not to try and hide in the building because there was a second-day belt line. There were stories about nails and chains in the belts on the second day. I didn't know if this were true, but I opted for the first-day belting.

Two bullies grabbed me as I stepped out the front door and pulled me to the head of the line. They shoved me in, and I ran and screamed like a bat out of Joplin. (I had been told to cry and yell to make them think they'd achieved their goal of ultimate torture.) I was a fast runner, but I caught enough licks on the side of my face, neck, and back—I'd forgotten to pad my back. The line seemed eternally long. When I finally came out, I made sure to yell louder than normal, which didn't take much effort, and I didn't have to make myself cry as I turned to let them see my tears. I had no pride; I only wanted to be sure they felt gratified and wouldn't make me run through again.

I started for home, wishing for the solitude, quiet, and emptiness of the Bootheel. Fink and the belt line were an awful lot to endure in one day. Life couldn't get much worse. Fortunately, I had a quarter in my pocket, so I went by the drugstore, bought a Mr. Goodbar, and ate it slowly on the way home.

The seventh grade was the longest year of my life. That fall I was introduced to more strange things—grown-up things and cruelties that couldn't be explained, like my first encounter with Old Joe the Bottle Man.

It was sometime in October. I was walking home down the Southern Railroad shortcut with about fourteen other boys, trying to be a part of the gang, when one of them spotted him and shouted, "There's Old Joe; let's go get 'im!"

Old Joe was a poor old black man who collected milk bottles, Coke bottles, and fruit jars in a tow sack to sell at the junk yard. I had heard what boys did to him, and now I was caught up in the middle of it. They started running toward him and screaming like Indians in a cowboy movie; I sort of jogged along, too afraid and embarrassed to do otherwise. He didn't see the pack until they got very close. Then he dropped his sack and ran into an old gray house near the tracks as the boys picked up stones and brickbats and smashed his sack of bottles. While I watched empty-handed, I saw a larger boy look at me pointedly. I picked up a rock and threw it, making sure it didn't hit the sack; no one was the wiser.

When all his bottles were broken, they stopped cheering and yelling and went on home. When my mother got home from work, I told her what had happened and asked her why those boys do such a thing. She consoled me and agreed it was a terrible thing, but she had no answer.

The next day, I decided not to take the Southern shortcut, but that meant I would most likely run into Change-for-a-Penny. He was an ageless little bent white man, not quite five feet tall, with an extremely large bottom lip. He wore an old brown hat and carried what looked like a doctor's black satchel. He lived somewhere near Bellevue and continually walked the four block area around the school. The students knew him and would call out, "Hey, got change for a penny?" His answer was always several minutes of loud profanities and incomprehensible mutterings. The students would disappear while he still yelled. Once he would stop, someone else would yell, "Hey, got change for a penny?" and it would start all over again. I asked my mother about this, too, but she didn't understand it, either. There was a boy in the ninth grade who had beaten up several of the taunters because Change-for-a-Penny was his uncle. The boy lived in a nice two-story house on Peabody Avenue.

Occasionally I went home yet another route, cutting across a vacant lot by myself. One day I heard a police car turn into the middle of the lot. It stopped suddenly, and a policeman jumped out and started chasing a young black man. He tackled him in the middle of the field, took his billy club, and hit him. He kept hitting him and hitting him while the black man screamed. When the black man stopped screaming, the policeman looked up and saw me. He stared at me harshly, so I walked away. When I got to the edge of the lot, I looked back and saw the policeman still looking down at the broken man.

But all was not that terrible that year, because anytime I could get a dime, I could go to the Linden Circle Picture Show and see a double feature. Or if I happened to be completely out of money, I could go to the Linden Circle Drugstore and watch the rich boys play the pinball machines.

There was one boy named Danny Bolton, a ninth-grader, that we believed to be very rich because he had as many as four different sweaters and he played the pinball machine every day. Sometimes we poor broke boys would watch him for hours as he fed up to a dollar and a half into the machine. One day I was with a group of about ten other boys standing outside the drugstore when Danny started boasting about how much money his daddy made and making fun of at least half of us who had no money at all.

"Look at this, you poor boys," he said, pulling a handful of change out of his pocket. Then he held up a shiny coin and said, "See this nickel? I have so much money that I can throw this nickel away." We watched in disbelief as he threw it across Linden Avenue into an open field and challenged all us poor boys to go look for it in the grass. No one was that poor. However, I did mark carefully where it landed, calculating its location at a point on an imaginary line between the sidewalk and a pole in the field.

"Some of you poor boys will be going over there to get that nickel," Danny predicted with the confidence of the rich before he turned on his expensive heel and left.

However, none of the agonies of not having much money or of seeing unexplained injustices were as hard as having Miss

Fink and the terrible stigma and kidding that accompanied that misfortune. She was a Memphis-wide legend, and seldom a day passed when I didn't hear some invisible chorus chanting *Sophye Olive Hot Tamale Inky Stinky FINK.* It was not unusual to run into a group of boys I didn't even know and hear one of them say with a sneer, "Hey, there's one of Fink's." Nearly anywhere I spent any money, an older kid would appear from nowhere and warn, "Better not spend all your money. Remember, you have to bank a nickel Monday."

Actually I did quite well with banking, using a nickel of my hard-earned Bootheel money every week to save the horrendous embarrassment Miss Fink had threatened on the first day. There were a couple of occasions when I slipped up and got to school with only a dime for soup, but it was no great sacrifice to bank half my soup money and buy a five-cent chocolate eclair for lunch.

One morning in early March, my mother went to work early and left me a sack lunch instead of a dime for soup. I looked in three secret places where I thought I had money, but there was none. I couldn't find a nickel anywhere. My banking record was in great jeopardy. Suddenly it flashed in my mind that Danny Bolton's nickel was probably still in the field, which was four blocks out of my way. I ran through the mist to the drugstore, lined myself up just where we were standing a few months earlier, went straight across the dead grass, and in less than a minute found the coin shining up at me. It was as if the rain had washed it clean for me to find quickly. I grabbed it and ran all the way to school before the tardy bell rang. I was still a little wet as I hurried up to bank my nickel, and Miss Fink sent me to the rest room to dry off.

The rest of the spring passed with more of the same and always with strains of "Sophye Olive Hot Tamale Inky Stinky FINK" in the air. The week before school was out, Miss Fink announced that all but four students had made the Thrifty Honor Roll and that the reward for the faithful would be a picnic and a trip to the Overton Park Zoo. She called out the names of the four who had failed to be thrifty and made them stand in front of the class while she read off all the wonderful things the rest of us would do.

About a week later, the day before the last day of school, we all gathered in front of the building where several mothers had come in three cars and a pickup truck to carry us to our reward. Naturally, everyone tried to pile in the back of the pickup. I was the first one in and held my ground. Miss Fink had to make several get out and ride in the cars.

The truck led the way. Miss Fink had instructed us to sit at all times, but just as we pulled out, Barbara Mitchell stood up and started to fall off the back of the truck. I leaped and grabbed her ankles so that she hung backwards by her knees from the tailgate. Everyone was screaming, but the driver thought that was normal for a truckload of seventh-graders on an outing. We went a block with Barbara dangling before the driver finally caught on and stopped the truck. I held on till someone got her down. She seemed very stunned and slightly unconscious. Everyone was shocked. One of the mothers put her in a car and took her to the doctor. The rest of us went with dampened spirits to the picnic.

At the park we tried to play some games while the adults set the marvelous home-cooked food on the tables. Things were going pretty slow when a car drove up and out stepped Barbara and her daddy, who just happened to be a doctor. She merely had a bump on her head and was all right. In a few minutes Dr. Mitchell, Miss Fink, and two of the mothers came over to where I was tossing a softball.

"This is the young boy who did the heroic deed," Miss Fink proclaimed. Then Barbara's daddy said several complimentary things, took out his billfold, and gave me two brand new dollar bills. Everyone gathered around me, and I was getting more attention than I had in many years. I noticed that Miss Fink's wig had shifted in the excitement as she shouted, "You see, Alvin, it really pays to be thrifty!" She wasn't smiling—she never smiled—but she had a different look in her eyes.

I remained the center of attention while we stuffed for an hour and a half on fried chicken, potato salad, homemade ice cream and cake. Then we all went to the zoo, where we rode the ponies, saw the lions and tigers, fed the monkeys and other animals, and had a wonderful day in spite of Miss Fink's presence. At least twice when I ran by her, she repeated, "It pays to be thrifty!"

Toward the end of the day, we were all waiting outside the birdhouse, watching the peacocks run loose, when from a distance through the trees and animal sounds some voices sang out, *Sophye Olive Hot Tamale Inky Stinky FINK.* She didn't seem to hear it. She never seemed to hear it.

11

Wild Dewberries

THE SUMMER BEFORE I turned fourteen, my daddy carried me to my Grandmother Bradie's to stay a few days. That summer she and Grandfather had just moved to Jabbo Nichol's farm, about a mile north of Tyler, halfway between Cooter and Cottonwood Point.

As Daddy turned a corner to go the last little distance to my grandparents' home, we passed a house near the road. I looked back and saw a blond-headed girl running through a grove of young trees to catch a glimpse of our car. There still weren't many automobiles on the road between Cooter and Cottonwood Point.

We went on to Grandmother's new home, which was much bigger than her previous one and had a lot of rooms. The house was already full of relatives. Grandmother said I could stay for a while, but I'd have to sleep on a pallet in my uncles' room. Uncle T.L. and Uncle Charlie were yet unmarried and still lived at home with their parents. T.L., in his early twenties, was a tall, good-looking, hard-working ladies' man with an entertaining sense of humor. He had coal black hair and sharp features. Charlie, who was nearly ten years older, complained of asthma all the time, didn't work much, and was losing his hair. He was very moral. That first night in T.L. and Charlie's room went pretty well except that Uncle Charlie snored all night long.

The next morning, Mrs. Howard, who lived in the house we passed on the corner, came up the road with her young daughter. Everyone gathered on the front porch, where Grandmother was snapping beans. I wandered out and Grandmother introduced me as "Carrie's boy," and I met Mrs. Howard's daughter, Teresa Peaches.

Right away I noticed that Teresa Peaches was very round all over—not fat, but very round. After a while, we wandered away from the grown-ups to the back yard, where we talked about chickens and cows. She told me she'd be sixteen in January. Again I observed that she was very healthy and impressively round. I was reminded of several of my young aunts who had small babies. Some of them would retire to a back room to nurse their babies, but some would feed on the spur of the moment regardless of who was in the room. Aunt Irene, who was about twenty, had a baby, and all the young boys in the family always hoped she wouldn't retire to the back to nurse because she was a lovely woman. Teresa Peaches looked as if she'd make some baby a wonderful mother some day.

When we exhausted the subject of chickens and cows, I found out that she'd never been to Memphis, so I began to talk about its tall buildings, the zoo, and the moving picture shows. Then I told her about the hills in western Tennessee and exaggerated their grandeur. She seemed impressed, for an older girl, and told me she'd never seen a building higher than three stories *or* a mountain and that she hoped to see a mountain some day. She talked a lot about their new battery radio (there was still no electricity in the Bootheel) and the fact that she had decided she wanted to be a singer. "Everybody tells me that I sing well," she said.

I bragged a little about my ability to make two dollars and fifty cents a week carrying water to the field hands and showed her some of my money—not all of it; I was pretty shrewd about my money. I told her we could go get some Co'Colas at the Tyler store if she had time some day. She said I could call her "Peaches" and she'd ask her mother about going to the store. We went back to the front just as Mrs. Howard was beginning to step down from the porch. I walked to the edge of the yard with them, and

Mrs. Howard said they would be canning the next day but that we could go to the store the day after that.

So I went down to the corner to meet Peaches early in the afternoon the day after they canned. We left our shoes on her front porch but soon came back after them because there were no clouds to shade the dusty road that burned our feet.

During the mile walk to the store, we fell into a sort of competition of who could tell the most exciting information about our respective worlds. I told her about the Sterick Building in Memphis. "It's twenty-nine stories high. From the top on the south side you can see parts of Mississippi, Tennessee, and Arkansas. On the other side, you can see Tennessee, Missouri, and Arkansas."

She jumped in front of me and asked, "Do you know that you can never leave a dead person in a window without a screen?" I shook my head no. "Cats will eat the nose off any corpse," she explained matter-of-factly. "A family between here and Cottonwood Point put a body on the second floor and left it in a window without a screen, and the next morning the nose was plumb gone!"

"Last year a man jumped off the Harahan Bridge into the Mississippi River," I said. "I was there with thousands of other people who came to watch. He jumped off wearing a football helmet and a swimming suit, just for fun. And he survived. Most people couldn't do that; the fall would kill you."

"Have you ever seen a mad dog?" she asked, jumping in front of me again. I shook my head no, but I'm sure she saw the fear that came into my face at the mere mention of mad dogs. "Well, I saw one last summer biting a fence post," she said. "That old cur was biting everything in sight. I ran and got my daddy, and he shot it between the eyes."

I told her about all the animals I had seen at the Memphis Zoo.

"Did you ever see anyone have a baby?" she asked.

"No," I said, hoping she hadn't either.

"Well, I never actually saw anyone have a baby, but year before last, I heard it. Katie who lives down the road from us had a baby, and the doctor was late getting there. I could hear her screaming from across the cotton fields. It was terrible. My parents turned up the radio so I couldn't hear it." Then she went into detail about what she'd heard about the agonies of childbirth. I didn't really want to hear it.

About halfway to the store, we passed a small woods lot. She stopped quick and said, "That's Halfway Woods Lot. That's where they do it." I pretended not to hear and said I'd seen a moving picture called "The Invisible Man" at Loew's Palace in Memphis. I tried to impress her with how scary it was and that I had to walk seven blocks home in the dark when it was over, and I was only eight years old at the time. That kept her quiet and thinking for a few minutes.

Then, just before we got to the store, she jumped in front of me and announced, "I'm going to tell you something I haven't told many people. One night last year, I was out on the back porch, and I saw a red devil in a rocking chair go across the sky. Nobody believes it. I told my mother, and she just laughed."

"How big was it?" I asked.

"It was big. It was just a big red devil, and it rocked across the sky and disappeared."

I figured there was no way I could whip her at this story-telling. For a while I wouldn't have to try, since we had reached the store. It was a big old dark country store; the ceiling was about twenty feet high and the big room went back forty feet. Several old men sat on a bench beside the door. There were bins of grain, rice, and beans and big stacks of flour in sacks and yellow stands of lard. The dry goods were to one side—cloth, overalls, shoes, straw hats. The cold drinks were in a big metal cooler near the cash register. We got to stick our arms down in the melting ice and fish around a long time to find what we wanted from among the RCs, Pepsis, Orange Crushes, and peach sodas. (When people in the Bootheel said they were "goin' to get a Co'Cola," they usually got some other kind of cold drink.)

After we'd cooled off our arms and picked out our drinks, we got a couple of Baby Ruths and started slowly back toward home, telling stories.

When we got to Halfway Woods Lot again, she turned and jumped in front of me and said, "That's where they do it, Alvin."

This time I didn't know how to evade her announcement. "What are you talking about?" I asked.

"That's where the two whores come once a month. I heard my daddy talking about it. It's terrible. And do you know the most terrible thing? They're a mother and daughter. And the other thing, Alvin, is you can't tell 'em apart. They're the same size and look the same age. Only terrible men go in there on the Saturday nights that those two whores are there. They go back into the woods lot and do evil."

This explained what Uncle Charlie and Uncle T.L. were always arguing about. I had heard Uncle Charlie tell Uncle T.L. that he'd better stay away from Halfway Woods Lot. I never knew for sure what they were talking about before; they would usually go out to the corner of the yard to finish their fussing so I couldn't hear.

Suddenly, while I was figuring all this out, Peaches turned and ran back to the woods lot, so I followed. It was no bigger than a large yard and had twenty or thirty trees spaced about twenty feet apart. There were wagon and car tracks winding all through the trees. As I wandered around looking at the ground, Peaches appeared abruptly, put her hands quickly and firmly on my shoulders, and pushed me down to the ground, saying, "You sit there." Then she jumped up on a stump and announced, "I'm gonna sing for you." She started with "When They Ring Those Golden Bells for You and Me" and introduced her next number saying, "This is my best song; everyone likes this best. It's 'Mother, Queen of my Heart.'"

She had a strong—even beautiful—alto voice and sang each song with such emotion that I applauded enthusiastically for her. When Peaches let go with "When the Moon Comes over the Mountain," I was actually starting to think she was as good as Kate Smith. The timber shook with that one, but I'm sure there was no one else within hearing distance but me. And, while she entertained me, I noted that she was rounder than my old friend Martha Sue or even the Whitney sisters or any other girl in the Bootheel.

All at once the performance was over, and she jumped off her stump-stage and ran down the road with me following behind. When I caught up with her, we continued to walk and talk until she again jumped in front of me and demanded, "Have you ever done it, Alvin?"

I hemmed and hawed—I couldn't lie but I was embarrassed to give her a straight answer. I said some things about Martha Sue and the Whitney sisters, and somehow she concluded that I hadn't done it. "Well, I haven't either," she said, "but I could have, and I almost have, and it won't be long because Henry is going to marry me."

I had heard at Grandmother's the night before that Henry had his eye on Peaches. He was known around the Bootheel as the best tractor driver in the world. There were only three or four tractors in that area, but even my uncles agreed that he took up to a tractor real well. They had seen him make a tractor rear up at the end of a field row and set it back down facing the opposite direction on the very next row.

"Yes, Henry's gonna marry me," she went on. "He's the best tractor driver in the world, and he's already talked to my daddy. Daddy said I'd have to be at least sixteen before he'd even consider it, but Henry's gonna carry me to the County Fair in Caruthersville this fall." She hesitated for a while, then she jumped in front of me again and said, "When I do get married, I'm gonna have lots and lots of babies."

She scared me to death.

By that time, we were at her house. She ran up to the porch, and I walked on to Grandmother's.

Two days later, Peaches walked up to Grandmother's and asked if I would like to go pick wild dewberries. I said I would, and she instructed me to bring two buckets to her house that afternoon. When I got there, she came out with two buckets, one containing a pint fruit jar filled with her mother's secret chigger repellent. She opened it up for me to inspect and said, "This will keep us from getting eaten up with chiggers, but we won't need to put it on till we get to where they're real bad." It was a white, pasty salve that smelled and looked like kerosene mixed with flour.

Since it was cloudy, we left our shoes on her porch and had no trouble touching our bare feet to the road. As we left, Mrs.

Howard hollered after us, "Watch out for storms, now. Come home if it gets bad."

Our route took us by Halfway Woods Lot again, and as we passed it, Peaches couldn't help saying, "That's where they do it, Alvin." I didn't respond. We turned left and went on down a less-traveled road about a half a mile to where it dead-ended. We climbed over a locked wooden gate and took a diagonal path up the levee.

The top of the levee was a dramatic place in that part of the world. It wasn't very high, but you could see out some distance. Just being up thirty feet was something. The only comparable thing in the area was the Indian mound on the other side of Cottonwood Point. We stood there and mused for a while. Thunder rumbled and we could see some distant darkness back in the West, but it didn't seem dangerous. So we went down to the land between the river and the levee. She told me she had seen water lapping over the top of the levee during the big flood.

The bottom land was full of lush growth and enormous trees. "This is the way all of this land was before the levee was put up," Peaches said. And for the first time I tried to imagine the whole Bootheel as this kind of Eden. Uncle Will had told me that everything used to be under water before the swampy land was drained, but it had never seemed real to me before.

We walked on for about ten minutes, meandering among the shade trees and backwash pools to where the dewberries grew. We were pretty far back under the trees on a slightly risen flat area when she said, "We've got to put on our chigger salve now." And as suddenly as a summer rainstorm, she flicked off her lilac dress and stood there in her white bloomers rubbing salve all over her roundness. She poured some of the salve into my hands and told me to take off my shirt and rub it in. Then I had to put some on her back. Nothing was said from then on. She took off her bloomers and there, bare under the trees, we did it.

Afterwards, we found many large, lush berries and filled our buckets. She took a handful and washed them in a pool, blew on them to make sure there were no remaining spider eggs in them, and gave half to me. We ate them and smiled.

The thunder sounded closer, so we started running toward home. When we passed Halfway Woods Lot, she couldn't help saying, "That's where they do it." We could see the rain maybe five miles away. The storms never reached the farm that night, but there were thunder and lightning all around the county.

Peaches and I picked wild dewberries two more times before Daddy came to carry me back to Aunt Annie's. As we turned the corner at the Howard house, I saw her run out and dash among the young trees. She jumped up on the pump house and waved at me as we disappeared in the dust. That was my last full summer in the Bootheel.

Back in Memphis during the winter, my mother got a newsy letter from Grandmother saying that Henry was going to marry Peaches and that Uncle T.L.was really bad off with some unknown sickness.

The next summer I stayed with Mother in Memphis and worked. In midsummer we took a quick trip to my Grandmother's. After we arrived and greeted everyone, Mrs. Howard and Peaches walked up to visit, too. We had already talked about Peaches and Henry being married. I smiled at her a couple of times as the grown-ups talked, and she smiled back.

After a while, we both went back by the smokehouse to see Tinny and her new puppies, and Peaches said, "I'm going to have a baby, Alvin. Isn't that wonderful?" Then she put my hand on the small roundness of her tummy. I felt a little funny because I'd never even met Henry.

Mother and I went back to Memphis that afternoon.

My grandparents moved to Point Pleasant in the northern part of the Bootheel the next year, and I didn't visit them much anymore. But in the summer of 1944, just before I was drafted into the Navy, I borrowed a car, got some black market gas, and went into the Bootheel. I drove all around and visited many of my relatives. My last visit was with Mr. Rushing at the Tyler Store. He told me that Peaches and her husband Henry, who turned out to be 4-F, had moved to work in a war plant up near St. Louis. Then he said that Uncle T.L. had died of syphilis after losing his mind. The family had kept that news from me.

On the way back to the main road, which was now graveled, I passed the Halfway Woods Lot, where they had all done it. No one was in sight. It was a normal summer day—looked as if it might storm. I didn't wander over the levee, but I knew lots of wild dewberries waited there for those who had the time and the chigger salve.

12

The Elmwood Route

ALMOST EVERY FIFTEEN-YEAR-old boy in Memphis looked forward to the day he'd turn sixteen with the hope that he could get a paper route and become "a *Commercial Appeal* boy." When I was fifteen and a half, I went down to the Number Five Paper Pick-up Station and talked to Mr. Ketcher, the district manager. He told me he'd give me an application when I got a twenty-five-dollar bond. I got one and he said he'd do his best to put me to work when I came of age in November.

I had heard from other paper boys at school that almost every new carrier had to start with the Elmwood route, the one nobody wanted. It was bounded, except for one throw, by the main line of the old Southern Railroad on the south, a spur of the Southern on the north, and Neptune and East streets on the west and east. On these streets and in between was the toughest, darkest, scariest part of town. The route was named for Elmwood Cemetery, which was just south of the main Southern line. A narrow, arched concrete bridge led from Dudley into the cemetery. The carrier had to throw a paper at the caretaker's house about an eighth of a mile into the tombstones. No one had ever stayed with it for over two months.

Veteran paper boys would warn prospective newcomers about the ethnic makeup of the Elmwood route. Of the one hundred fourteen customers, only eight were white; ten were Chinese, ninety-six were black, and none of them liked paper boys who came collecting bills. There was no way to break even on that route, they said. And they always threw in some kind of terrifying story about the morphodite on Elliot Street.

My desire to become a *Commercial Appeal* boy and bring in some steady money was stronger than the fears these stories roused. So, two weeks before my sixteenth birthday in November of 1941, I went back to see old Mr. Ketcher, who was probably about forty-five at the time. He was sort of a snakey, thin man who had a 4-F classification for no obvious reason. He didn't look unhealthy; neither did he look very wholesome—sort of a Fagan type. He never took off his dress felt hat. His beady black eyes never looked at me as he told me to show up early on the first of December to throw the Elmwood route.

It was customary for a new boy to have a guide with him his first day, but Ketcher had been throwing the route himself for a week and was evidently tired of it. He just gave me the papers with a list of addresses, drew a crude map, and said, "Do the best you can."

So I took off into the darkness alone at three o'clock in the morning. It was a neglected area. The street lights stood two or three blocks apart, each giving only a faint glimmer from a single weak bulb. I was careful to walk down the middle of the street as I searched for my addresses and heaved the papers up onto the small, dilapidated stoops. All the yards were at least five steps up from the street, and most of the houses had three more steps up to their doors, creating an atmosphere that must have been exactly like the Valley of the Shadow of Death, I thought. By the time I got to the cemetery, I felt almost relieved to be there. I figured dead people were harmless most of the time.

It took me three hours to deliver all my papers that first morning, but I survived. By the end of the week, I had learned the route and felt pretty good. On that Saturday, I waited till the sun was well up to collect for my first weekly bill. All but eight customers paid their twenty-five cents, and I cleared nine dollars.

By the end of the first month, I had decided I was going to make it. I established a routine of getting up every morning at two-fifteen and using the newly-invented pancake mix to fry me up a stack to eat with molasses before braving the cold and dark. Although it was a lonely, tiring, spooky job, I began to savor the mysterious silence punctuated by occasional night sounds and strange and wonderful smells that dissipated with the day. Life in the city between three and four in the morning was different. I moved through utter darkness, memorizing the location of potholes, while most of the population slept. Even the milk wagons didn't start until after four. One morning as I walked to the pick-up station, the wind blew from just the right northerly direction and the city was so dead that I could hear the lions roaring from the Memphis Zoo about four miles away. And there were mornings when the delicious smell of boiling cottonseed oil made me forget the pancakes I'd just eaten and think I was starving.

At the Southern Railroad, I found a consistent bright spot on the dark route. Chester, the train gate operator, sat in a little tower about twenty feet high. I'd crawl up the ladder to hand him his paper, and he'd always smile at me like a normal human. Soon he started asking me to come into his tiny room and warm up by his little bitty pot-bellied stove. He was a quiet old man, about sixty-five, who laughed a lot and chewed tobacco and spat in a big can in the corner. Almost every morning, we'd visit for ten minutes in the dim lantern light, and I would watch, fascinated, as he lowered and raised the four train gates with his levers. I never got to know him very well—we only talked about general things—but his friendly presence was a big relief to me, and it occurred to me years later that he was probably just as grateful for me as I was for him.

I usually didn't encounter any of my other customers unless I was collecting, but one January morning just after I had thrown a paper at the door of a comparatively well-kept house, I heard a woman's voice call out from the darkness, "Paper boy!"

I jumped, turned around, and answered as politely as I could, "Yes, ma'am?"

"Come up here," the voice called.

Cautiously I climbed the ten wooden steps up to the door, where a black lady in a clean, starched dress and apron stood, fat and smiling. "Would you like a biscuit and jelly?" she asked, as friendly as Aunt Annie.

"Yes, ma'am," I said.

"You wait here, paper boy; I'll be right back." In a little bit, she returned with a biscuit half as big as a dinner plate and filled with blackberry jam and butter. She handed it to me on a piece of cardboard. "This will make you get through the morning real good."

"I sure thank you, ma'am." I walked down the street a few houses, sat on the curb, and devoured my unexpected prize. The huge biscuit was hot and fluffy with a buttery, crusty top, and I licked up the jam and melted butter that was oozing from its split middle. I enjoyed every crumb in the feeble light of a street lamp while I wondered how many people had to survive by wandering through the dark.

The next day, I told Chester about the nice black woman. "Yeah, there are some good folks back in there," he confirmed, "and there are some mean, bad folks, too."

Every morning after that for months to come, I never failed to fold the nice black lady's paper extra hard and throw it at her door with as much force as the vision of a hot biscuit and jam could summon. For four days, I hit the screen with a rousing thwack and turned to walk slowly out of hearing distance, but she didn't appear. Maybe she didn't want to overdo it, I thought, or maybe the biscuits weren't ready when I came. Then one morning she poked her head out the door and asked, "Would you like another biscuit?"

For a while, I couldn't figure the pattern of these lucky days. But after several weeks, she began to ask me in to eat my biscuit, and I learned that her husband, a railroad worker, had to get to work early on some days, and those were the days I got to share his breakfast. Her name was Miss Maggie, and she must have fed me fifty biscuits during the two years I threw her paper.

I really didn't have the trouble with customers that other carriers had warned me about. There were a few who told me they didn't have the money when I first went by to collect. I simply asked them when they would and kept going back till they paid. I never got ugly with them or threatened to cut off their papers. I just treated them the same as I would have treated the rich folks on Peabody. It didn't take them over a month to realize this, and they started scraping up their quarters on time every Saturday. None of them ever robbed me or threatened me or gave me good cause to be afraid—except for the morphodite on Elliot Street, who grabbed me once and scared the fire out of me.

Actually, it only grabbed my bags. When it called me onto the porch of its little shotgun shack one pitch dark morning and I got close enough to see its clownish, made-up face inviting me to "Come on in here," I turned and ran. I could feel it tugging the straps on my bags and repeating in an unnaturally feminine whine, "Come on in here a while," but I pulled loose and dashed back to the middle of the street. As always, I walked cautiously and never relaxed until I got to the cemetery.

The thing I feared most on the route—or anywhere in Memphis—were the gangs of white hoodlums who terrorized young boys out of whatever money they might have. I had first seen what they could do while I was walking home from the Linden Circle Movie Theater one night when I was twelve. I was a few yards behind Terry Greenway and his friend when I heard tires screeching about two blocks behind us. I jumped into some hedges and watched two cars pull up. Eight thugs got out, grabbed the boys, and demanded their money. One boy gave them everything, but Terry said, "No." Charlie Bowman, the boss, got out and asked Terry his name. Then he told three of them to "hold him." Charlie braced himself and spat on his hand, giving Terry time to realize what was going to happen. Then he said, "Now, turn him loose," and he hit Terry's face with the side of his fist, knocking him down. He did that five or six times. Then one of the holders said, "Let me hit him, Charlie." So Charlie let his helper have a hit, but he didn't use the side of his fist and his hand came back bleeding. Charlie cursed him and shouted, "Don't mess up your knuckles on the runt!"

I was so mortified that I ran home, often hiding behind trees and telephone poles to make sure the coast was clear. When I saw Terry again, his personality was shattered. "Never get caught" became my motto, and it was always on my mind as I walked down the dark streets of the Elmwood route. I was careless one morning and Charlie's gang did catch me, but I had only thirty cents, so they let me go.

Mean old Mr. Ketcher was my next biggest pain. He loved to collect fines: five dollars for not completing a route on time (six a.m.) and fifty cents per customer complaint. I was never late; I got home before light even in the summer. And I knew my people would never rat on me. So when I got my first complaint fine, I called Ketcher on it. I told him I had talked to all my customers and no one had called him. He let up on me some. He was known to create complaints by driving by and picking up papers off porches.

Then there was always the weather. The most terrifying morning I remember started out in a pouring rain. I put on my slicker but was soaked to the skin by the time I got to the pick-up station. When I crossed the Southern tracks to start down Neptune, I saw that water was beginning to stand in the streets.

I made it to Chester's and climbed up the ladder. "Look," he said, "the water is flowing down the tracks like a river. You'd better wait it out here. It looks like a flood." I waited there fifteen minutes, but the water only got higher. I figured I'd miss my six o'clock deadline if I waited much longer—or worse, I'd be unable to get through the rest of the route at all and be fined five dollars. So I walked on in the dark with water up to my ankles and sometimes my knees. There were no biscuits at Miss Maggie's. "Bad luck," I thought as a new cloudburst pelted the rain down even harder. I threw the cemetery's paper and came back to throw East and Dudley streets, which I couldn't see for the water. When I finally made it back to the Southern Yard and looked east, water was flowing west just over the tops of the four tracks, which were built up about three feet high. I was cold and wet and bumfuzzled and afraid I couldn't get home, which was about a mile east up the tracks.

I decided I could make it by walking between the tracks and holding on to the ends of the crossties. The water was rushing hard, and I stumbled a few times as the rain continued to pelt me. Then, about halfway to the place where I turned off the tracks for home, I saw a train headlight approaching. No problem, I thought, as long as I'm not on the track. There was enough space between the tracks for two trains to pass each other with about three feet to spare. Normally, I'd just cross over the tracks and wait. But I grew mortally afraid because I couldn't tell which track it was on. As it got closer, the light blinded me, and I couldn't see or think. I kept telling myself I'd be okay as long as I wasn't on the track, but it was hard to stand steady in the rushing water. I decided to squat. Just as I did, something told me to look around—and there was a train coming from the other direction.

I could do nothing but try to keep my head above the churning, elevated water and within the three clear feet between the trains as they sped by, creating a violent river. I fought the water and imagined the waves throwing me onto the track where I could be cut in half. Then, as rapidly as they had snuck up on me, they disappeared. The last of the big waves died, and I found a crosstie to hang on to as I tried to regain my balance.

I made my way on down the tracks to the Memphis Furniture Company, where I heaved myself over the two north tracks and walked the short distance up the alley to our house. At home everything was normal. My mother didn't bother me with questions. I dried off and got ready for school, glad that I hadn't drowned or been cut in half or caught by the police, who often patrolled the tracks to keep illegal rail walkers out of harm's way.

The next week, Mr. Ketcher called me in and told me that I had kept the Elmwood route long enough. I had been throwing it for four months and had probably set a record. He offered me a new route on Union Avenue close to the Med Center with one hundred twenty customers.

I should have been elated—this was the big step up and out—but I felt that I really knew Elmwood and its customers, who depended on me. I had gotten used to its shadowy, depressed streets, to the fears, to the biscuits and jelly, and to Chester. I didn't want to give it up. "Has anyone ever been allowed to throw two routes?" I asked.

He immediately took me up on my offer and told me he'd drop off my papers for the second route where it began so I would only need one bag. I thought old Ketcher was actually being nice, but he was probably just glad to have a regular

Elmwood carrier and was afraid I'd come to my senses and back out.

Later on, I added another easy route. I was walking eleven miles every morning and bringing home thirty to forty dollars a week. I gave all the routes up in December of my senior year—two years after I had started—to concentrate on high school track. I wanted to become the world's greatest runner.

The Elmwood route had given me the confidence to set another record. I had really sort of fallen in love with Elmwood; it was so bad, it was good. I had found a strange kind of warmth there, and my young ego had bloomed because I had kept the notorious route longer than anyone. Even more amazing, I didn't get robbed or killed, and the morphodite didn't get me.

13

R. O.

IN LATE OCTOBER OF 1944, a very long troop train carried me and hundreds of other sailors from the Naval training station at Great Lakes, Illinois. None of the new recruits I had met at boot camp were on that train; I didn't know a soul. The train emptied into Camp Bradford, Virginia, a large embarkation center fifteen miles out from Norfolk on the shores of Chesapeake Bay.

Camp Bradford was huge, flat, windy, wet, and cold. It consisted of a few administration buildings, several mess halls, and the sailors' housing, which was thousands of tents linked by wooden walkways through the mud and water. Each tent accommodated three sailors, usually, and a small stove that could hold three pieces of coal. I was six foot two and could barely stand up in my tent.

Our only purpose there was to wait. Every day we reported to the Classification Building to see if our overseas assignments had come in. This meant standing in the line a quarter of a mile long to get checked off for checking in. It wasn't a happy situation: no one wanted to go overseas, and no one wanted to stay in Tent City. There was a lot of apathy and despondency in the cold, wet bleakness. The brass had to keep constant count of us because there had been so many AWOLs and suicides. That's why we had to muster seven times a day—before breakfast, after breakfast, midmorning, before lunch, after lunch, midafternoon, and after supper. And it gave everybody something to do all day.

I was standing in classification line one day after two weeks of this terrible routine when an officer called me out of line. He pointed to a comment on my papers that said I'd had a little art training at the Memphis Academy of Art and that I'd be interested in working in art after the war. "What does this mean?" he asked. I told him it meant that I liked art. He turned and talked to another officer. Then he told me to sit on a long bench in a big, empty room nearby and wait for orders.

"Well, sir, I'm supposed to muster in twenty-five minutes," I said.

"I will call headquarters; you will be relieved of mustering until you hear from us. I want you to sit over there against that wall until you hear from us."

"Do you mean I've been given an assignment, sir?"

"No."

"Have I done something wrong?"

"No. We need to look into some things. Just sit over there and wait for further orders."

So I sat on the bench. Sometimes I paced back and forth in front of it, but I was afraid to walk more than a few feet away. Three and a half hours later, the same officer came in and said, "Your temporary orders are to go eat chow and go to your tent. You don't have to muster tonight or later until you hear from us. Anytime you're not eating your meals, you are to sit at this bench."

"Have I done something wrong, sir?" I asked again.

"No, sailor, but I'm not at liberty to tell you anything else. Eat your meals, don't muster, stay here till five p.m. every day."

I walked to the mess hall and then picked my way down the wooden walkway into the middle of Tent City. Each tent was identified by a string of large white letters and numbers. I had not made a single friend in that mass of humanity, so I went straight to my tent.

One of the sailors who shared my tent had just shipped out. When I ducked in, the remaining tentmate, who was in his mid-twenties, sat staring into space. I sat down and stared into space, too. After a while, I blurted out, "Hey, you wanna talk?"

"Not much to talk about at Camp Bradford," he said, still staring.

"Well, I've had something happen here. You've been here for a while; maybe you can understand it." I told him what had happened that day.

"My God, they're after you for something! They've set this camp up to drive us insane so we'll do anything to get out of here. Haven't you heard the announcements every day at two o'clock?"

"Yeah, what's that all about?"

"You know what they say: 'Now hear this, now hear this; report to Building Six Fourteen if you are interested in special duty and immediate assignment.' I've been watching, and every day about forty people go down to Building Six Fourteen, and you never see them again. I've heard rumors that's how they get their frogmen. They've got more men here than they have regular assignments, so they muster them till they'd do anything to get out. Take my advice, Mac, and don't volunteer for anything. Whatever assignment you get through normal classification will be normal duty. Volunteers end up as frogmen or some other kind of suicide duty." Then he told me about some people who trained for volunteer duty: they were sent to Florida, where they practiced swimming with dynamite strapped to their backs out to a ship, attaching the dynamite to the ship, and swimming quickly away. "Don't volunteer for anything," he repeated.

The next day I reported to my bench and sat there all morning while hundreds of people walked by for assignments. At noon I walked over to the clerical section and asked a yeoman if I could go to lunch.

"Yes," he replied. "Your assignment is to eat and, when you're not eating, to be over there on that bench."

"Yes, sir." So I ate lunch and reported back that afternoon. I sat, squirmed, and paced while my body began to ache all over from just sitting and being tense. Just before five that afternoon, the yeoman came and said, "No change in your temporary orders. See you tomorrow."

I wandered back through the mud to supper, imagining all the horrible things that might be in store for me. The third day was the same. In the middle of the afternoon of the fourth day, the yeoman called my name across the room and said, "Report over here." When I did, he told me to go to Captain Greyson's office down the hall. At least something was happening.

I walked into Captain Greyson's office and saw a plumpish officer of medium height with glasses and slightly gray hair. He told me to sit and started asking me basic questions about school, habits, preferences in life, and the size of my family. After about half an hour, he said, "That's all. Report back to your bench."

"Sir, may I ask questions about what is going on with me?" I ventured.

"You certainly may not. Report back to the bench and we'll be back in touch with you."

So I went back to my bench till five. The next day was excruciating. Nothing happened. All day I imagined that my papers had been lost or that I had done something or said something wrong during my interview with Captain Greyson. It wasn't until mid afternoon of the sixth day that the yeoman called me again and told me to report to Captain Greyson's office. I went in and sat down. He sat quietly for at least ten minutes. Then he reared back in his chair and looked at me. "Did you ever break a window in Bellevue Junior High at Memphis?" he asked.

"Sir, I was with a group of boys in the ninth grade. One of the boys broke the window. Several of us were accused, but I did not do it."

"What does Archie Lane mean to you?"

"I knew a young lady in Memphis by that name, sir."

"What kind of lady was she?"

"Archie Lane was a rather notorious young lady who loved to expose her body."

"You mean she liked to take off her clothes?"

"I saw her take off her clothes on two occasions, sir."

"You're a pretty truthful fellow, aren't you?"

"Well... May I ask..."

"You may not ask. I ask the questions; you give the answers. You have no brothers or sisters, correct?"

"That is correct, sir."

"Why did you walk out in the middle of a symphony at the Ellis Auditorium in Memphis last year?" he asked with a superior look.

"Sir, I had to collect the money for the three paper routes I was throwing before it got dark. The concert was running long, so I had to leave before it was over." I must have looked as if I were going to ask how he knew this because, before I could say anything else, he pronounced, "I have the information. I ask the questions. You respond only with answers. Who is Juanita Jowers?"

"That is one of my girlfriends in Memphis, sir."

"Is she your best girlfriend, only girlfriend, one of many?"

"Best girlfriend."

"How many other girlfriends do you have?"

"I haven't kept exact count, sir." I answered tersely.

"Then you do have a severe temper?"

"I believe most people consider me to have a very mild temper."

"But you sound upset."

"Well, I'm over it now." I realized then that I was caught up in the intimidation of this questioning. I was determined not to volunteer for the unknown and figured I'd better keep my cool. I had played the game for a week; I could continue.

"Do you consider yourself mentally stable?" he asked.

"Sir, I would consider myself as stable as most people," I answered, making it a point to look at him. As I did, I noticed that he didn't look quite right in the eyes.

"Oh, you're going to give evasive answers from here on out."

"I don't know what's going on, sir."

"You're not supposed to know. Do you look forward to going to sea on a landing ship?"

"No, sir."

"Why did you join the Navy?"

"I was drafted." I said, trying to give short, honest answers with no emotion.

"Are you true to your country?"

"Yes, sir."

"Do you consider yourself trustworthy?"

"Yes, sir."

He reared back in his chair and looked at me for a while with those strange eyes. "Did anyone ever tell you that you have a sensitive mouth?"

"No, sir."

"You're such a nice, clean-cut young man. Are you a virtuous young man?"

I hesitated for a long time before I answered, "No, sir."

"Go have your evening chow and check back here at six-thirty."

So I trudged to the mess hall, looked out over the bay at the ships, and felt angry, afraid, and hurt. I didn't want to go out on one of those LSTs, and I didn't want to volunteer for the unknown. I was about as baffled and upset as an eighteen-year-old boy could be. I ate slowly and went back to my little bench. I was beginning to have personal feelings about that little bench; it looked sort of like a church pew, and no one else ever sat there. It was my pew; it had felt my sweat and had sent some serious pains through my body.

The building was almost deserted. I saw a couple of yeomen and a WAVE or two. After a few minutes, Captain Greyson called me into his office. I sat and watched as he thumbed through a stack of papers for at least fifteen minutes. He looked up at me and back down several times. Finally he asked, "Have you ever been caught stealing?"

"I have never stolen, sir."

"I have the power to give you an assignment that will keep you from going overseas at least temporarily. It is completely up to me to recommend you."

"I'm still not at liberty to ask what is going on, sir?"

"I'll give you more information shortly."

About that time, there was a loud explosion in the bay, possibly the Navy ships testing their guns. Whatever it was shook the building. "My goodness," he said and walked to the window. "Come over here and look."

We looked out into the dark and saw things exploding in the air. I noticed that he started leaning on me. I moved to the right. So did he. I went back to my seat. I felt very strange and remembered that there were very few people in the building with us.

"Do you swim?" he asked.

"I passed my swimming test, sir." I knew he was going to start talking about frogmen next.

"I have a nice beach house at Virginia Beach, only twenty miles from here. I think I'll recommend you for the special assignment. If you're lucky enough to get it, I'll invite you to come to the beach house next spring."

"I've heard Virginia Beach is very nice, sir," I said, carefully trying to be noncommittal without sounding noncommittal.

"This is what I have to offer you," he began, and seemed businesslike, though friendly. "We have a special assignment suitable for you, but I'm not at liberty to tell you what it is. I can only tell you that you will not be going off on an LST for some time. If you want the assignment, go to your tent and report back here at oh seven hundred with your mattress and gear."

"What would I be doing in this assignment, sir?"

"You are not to know that."

"Can you tell me anything?"

"Nothing. But I can tell you that you'll be better off than you are now and better off than you would be at sea."

"What should I do if I don't want it, sir?"

"Report to the classification yeoman and tell him you don't want it. If you do want it, report at the east end of this building with your gear; someone will meet you there."

"But where will I go?" I whined.

"I can't tell you. Either show up with your gear at the east end of the building or tell the yeoman you don't want to accept the assignment."

He dismissed me coolly and I went to my tent, where I lay awake thinking until four in the morning. By that time I had decided to take the assignment, but I couldn't figure out why.

I got up and put my stuff together; it made a pretty hefty load for a one-hundred-fifty-four-pound string bean. Anxiety had not squelched my appetite, so I went to morning chow and then wrestled my gear over to the east end of the Classification Building. At ten minutes after seven, Captain Greyson appeared on a little porch and saw me. Soon two Marines came out of the door behind him. He handed one of them some papers and said, "Escort this sailor to the Reproduction Unit."

I could only imagine what went on in a reproduction unit, and I started to wonder if those questions about my girlfriends had any direct relevance to my being chosen for it. Meanwhile, the Marines instructed me to walk between them. Both had loaded rifles. They marched me straight to the water, where we turned right and proceeded up the bay to two very long buildings with double barbed-wire fences around them. Inside the fence, they turned me over to two other Marines, who guided me into a long hallway of one of the buildings. They deposited me in a dark waiting room. One told me, "Wait here," and they left and closed the door.

I sat in utter silence for about half an hour, trying to anticipate what might happen next. Suddenly a large officer opened the door and asked me if I was who I was. "Come in here," he said. I went in there.

"I am Captain Bailey," he began. "I'm the executive officer of this unit, which for security reasons is called simply Building Twelve. When someone outside the fence asks us what we are, we say we are the Reproduction Unit. My duty for the rest of the day is to thoroughly indoctrinate you that top security is our priority. We make invasion terrain models here for all branches of the service in the war. We have information sometimes weeks, sometimes months before the invasion will take place. You were selected from thousands at Tent City because your record shows you have art training. Are you still only eighteen?"

"Yes, sir, but I'll be nineteen pretty soon."

"You are by far the youngest in our unit, but we're going to give you a shot at our work. You will be taking the place and sleeping in the bunk of a man who is in prison for not keeping his mouth shut. I tell you now it will be best if you talk as little as possible. If you keep your mouth shut and can do the work, then you can stay in the unit as long as it is a unit."

He looked me square in the eye and added, "I have the power to put you on an invasion barge leaving Chesapeake Bay within forty-eight hours."

He let that sink in for a few seconds before continuing his two-hour speech on the importance of security. He explained that vegetables were used as code names for islands to be invaded. "If you ever hear any real island names, put them completely out of your mind and use only vegetable names," he warned. I still didn't comprehend much of what he told me. I just said "yes, sir" and "no, sir" as he repeatedly emphasized security and the man in prison.

"The man you are replacing is the reason none of us can take short liberties into Norfolk anymore. One night in town he got drunk and leaked information that was damaging to an invasion." The officer pushed a button. A yeoman came in and led me out to a dogtrot between the two buildings and into the barracks, where he showed me the unfortunate drunk's bunk and introduced me to several men who looked at me a little strangely. One of them said, "Oh, you're Grady's replacement. Hope you don't wind up like he did."

I put up my sea bag and sat down on the bunk to wonder. Soon I got a message to report to Captain Bailey's office after lunch. His instructions so far had made me afraid to talk to anyone in the mess hall, which was a special one separate from Tent City. I was well on my way to becoming a noncommunicator. I got more indoctrination about security that afternoon and still more the next morning. Then I reported to a man named Joad for duties. He told me Grady had been a well-trained artist and the unit was composed of professional photographers, sculptors, painters, and commercial artists. "I'm sure old Captain Bailey has given you the vegetable routine."

"Yes."

"Well, we're working on Cabbage now," he laughed. "You'll find out what it really is soon enough."

I didn't laugh. I was serious about this assignment. They had radiators here that made real steam heat, and I didn't want to leave.

The unit worked in eight-hour shifts around the clock. I started out on the day shift in a state of confusion, trying to comprehend the mounds of information Joad had given me the day before. The information kept coming, and I struggled to understand what I was supposed to be doing. We worked in an enormous room at large tables that contained terrain models of islands, made of clay, wood, and rubber. I met most of the people on my shift that first morning. Some were serious. Others were talkative and kidded me about my Southern accent. There were only two other Southerners in the whole unit, they told me. Most were from New York, Boston, and Pennsylvania. They pegged me "Tennessee" and made comments about my youth and lack of training. The brass had picked me out of Tent City, they said, because they didn't have time to wait for a professional replacement to be processed through Washington, D.C.

For the first week, I set my mind to learning fast. I tried not to talk or make friends. I just worked, ate, slept, and kept my mouth shut. After two weeks, a man with a scar across his forehead approached me as I was finishing my shift and he was starting his. He wasn't a very big man; he had a friendly face, and the scar seemed to lend power to his appearance. He looked to be about forty and was probably the oldest man in the unit. "How are you doing, Tennessee?" he asked without a hint of mockery or intimidation.

"All right."

"Any problems?"

"No, sir."

"Well, you let me know if you have any problems."

I wanted to ask who he was, but I dared not ask anyone anything, so I observed him when I could. He slept six bunks over from me. About the only thing I noticed was that he had stacks of books and was always reading when he wasn't working. I started calling him Socrates, and he didn't seem to mind.

Two days later, he walked over to my corner of the table as I was finishing up my shift and asked how I was doing. "Okay,"

I said, "but I'm having a hard time with photogrammetry." We had to look at photographs of the island through stereoscopic glasses for a three-dimensional effect. I was having trouble getting the terrain accurate.

"Do you think you could work the four p.m. to midnight shift?"

"If that were my assignment, I could," I said.

He winked at me and said, "We'll see what we can do."

The next day my assignment was changed, and I worked the evening shift at the same table as the friendly man with the scar. I learned his name was R.O. Street. Without saying a word, he became my protector. R.O. knew everything. He may have just been a chief petty officer, but he ran the unit. I heard he'd turned down a commission because he liked his work. Everyone knew he was the best in the unit.

Even with R.O.'s subtle guidance, I was still worried about my job. Eight to ten of us worked together on one model, which was divided into segments. When the shift changed, the next group took over where we left off. When we finished a model, it would be cast in plaster and used to make more than a hundred rubber models that were then painted and sent out before the invasion to each ship involved. As I worked, I kept hearing Captain Bailey's admonition: "The lives of our invasion troops depend on the accuracy with which you reproduce every detail of these island models."

I tried to look cool and calm, but my trepidation must have shown through, to the amusement of some of the other workers. "Yeah, old Captain Bailey is a mean one, all right," one of them said not long after I changed shifts. "He's shipped out several people who couldn't make the grade—not just Grady the drunk. Have you noticed that picture of Frazier on the wall over there, Tennessee? We keep it there just to remind us what can happen if we goof up." I looked up from my work to where he nodded and saw a mug shot of a former reproduction sailor and underneath it the caption, "He came with a flash and went with a splash." While that sank into my addled brain, one of the others said, "No one knew what happened exactly. He just did wrong, did bad, couldn't do it, was shipped out."

After a few minutes, when no one was looking, R.O. came over and looked through my stereoscopic glasses at the section where I was working. He took some instruments and made a few minor corrections, saying, "You'll get it; you'll get it." I was too afraid even to say "thank you." I imagined we'd both get shipped out if anyone knew he was helping me.

About a week later, the doors to our workroom flew open, and everyone snapped to attention. Six admirals and almost-admirals had slipped in with no warning. I heard someone whisper, "My God, there's Halsey."

Captain Bailey put us at ease and told everyone to keep working as he escorted the brass from one table to the other. During the commotion, R.O. quietly pushed me down in his chair and took mine. Finally they came to our model, Cabbage. I commenced to fumble with R.O.'s instruments, trying not to mess up his work, when Bailey and the brass came directly to me. He asked me to stand back while he and Halsey and the others looked at R.O.'s section for a long time. Then Bailey put his arm around me and said, "You're doing a great job, kid."

They went on to R.O. Bailey explained that R.O. was the unit's superior artist. R.O. stood back while they inspected my work silently for a few moments. Halsey slapped R.O. on the shoulder and said, "Superior work, Chief." As they left, I looked up at R.O. and he winked at me.

Later, as we walked back to our bunks, I thanked R.O. for his help.

"That's all right, Tennessee," he said. "It's hard business and you're doing fine. You really learned a lesson in there tonight."

"I don't understand it, R.O. They thought my work was good, and I know some of my roads are very inaccurate."

"That's just it. They don't know how to read those models— not even Bailey."

By the next week, I had relaxed a little and my work was coming along, but Captain Greyson had been sending me notes, and I was getting a little antsy about them. I had gotten three already that said, "As soon as you get settled and get a liberty, remember I have invited you to my beach house." I put them all deep in my sea bag and didn't mention them to anyone until R.O. questioned me about my mood.

"You've been awfully quiet, Tennessee," he said while we were shaving one morning.

"Captain Bailey gave me a good indoctrination on security."

"Captain Bailey is right. But you act like there's a problem."

I looked around to be sure no one was within hearing. "Have you ever heard of Captain Greyson?" I almost whispered.

"Good Lord, is Captain Greyson after you, too?"

"He's sent me several notes asking me to visit his beach house. He made me think he was responsible for getting me this assignment. I don't know what to do."

"Listen, Tennessee, you played it right and got in here on your own. He's always harassing some young, scared boy. Just forget it; he doesn't have any authority over you once you're in here."

"Are you sure it's all right?"

"I'll take care of it; don't worry."

About five days later, I heard Captain Greyson had been shipped out to California.

Several weeks after Christmas, our unit shipped out for an unknown destination which turned out to be Oahu, Hawaii, where we could be closer to the Japanese front. There we worked on vegetables I later learned were really Angar, Chichajima, Okinawa, Hiroshima, and Nagasaki. My good friend R.O. looked out for me through the whole experience.

I tried to keep my schedule close to his. In the late afternoons, R.O. would usually wander off to a quiet beach with several books and read until dark. I'd tag along to sit and talk to him about his friends Goethe, Kierkegaard, and Nietzsche. He encouraged me to read several books of philosophy. Some were beyond me, but I'd ask him to explain them, and he would. We'd also discuss the war, death, women, and other vital things. I decided R.O. was the ideal intellectual person—almost faultless.

In the meantime, my own worth in the unit took a dramatic turn. The All-Navy Track Team was based at the University of Hawaii in Honolulu, and the coach had learned by checking the records of every new sailor on the island that I had been Tennessee's champion high school high and low hurdler. He contacted Captain Bailey to request my partial release from duties so that I could begin a training program. Bailey refused to release me until the admiral in command of the islands told him to.

So I was given some special privileges. I had flexible hours and was treated with implicit trust. I had the use of a unit truck to deliver mail, and I had keys to just about everything. Every day at noon, a truck picked me up and took me to the University for track training. The mystique and fear of "The Reproduction Unit" began to lift, and soon I felt completely comfortable in my new freedom and moderate fame. Things seemed to lighten up for everybody on Oahu. The brass must have felt the island was more secure than Norfolk, and we weren't watched as closely as we had been. Several of the slicker men in the unit found ways to finagle invitations to parties in Honolulu and would slip out to homes that were off limits. I never got invited, so I never went. I was more concerned with my track duty, anyway.

I usually went in to work early so I could get six or seven hours in by noon. One morning just after sunup as I approached our work building, I saw a car pull up and dump a body at the feet of the Marine who guarded the building. When I got closer, I saw the body was R.O. The Marine just stared at him and said, "What is this?" I bent down and felt R.O.'s pulse. "He's alive," I said, "just dead drunk. I can't believe it. This man has gone through the war without making one mistake. We've got to do something before he gets found out."

I unlocked a storage area, and the Marine helped me drag R.O. in and pull him up to the sink. I took some towels and washed the dried vomit off his face, and he vomited again, still unconscious. I got the word out that R.O. was in bad shape and we'd have to cover for him. I didn't go in for track practice that day but stayed with R.O. in the storage room, trying to nurse him back to life. A couple of guys pulled double duty for us, and nobody who mattered noticed we were gone.

About four that afternoon, he came to and tried to joke a little. He explained that he had sneaked out to a party where he must have gotten hold of some bad whiskey—torpedo juice, they called it. It was a bootleg beverage made by taking the alcohol from a torpedo and straining it through bread.

After five, when I figured all the officers had left, I found a gurney and wheeled R.O. through secret passages to the barracks. The next day he was officially reported sick. A few nights later, when he was almost back to his full strength, we sat talking on a high bluff overlooking the ocean. "Even Socrates made mistakes sometimes," I thought out loud, trying to work through this nearly fatal mistake my protector had made.

"Old Socrates sure made a mistake this time," R.O. confessed without much remorse. "You know, you've got something to learn from this, too. Eventually all people will disappoint you in some way."

"That's depressing," I said, not ready to admit that I was disappointed.

"It's not that depressing. Look at it this way: if I hadn't messed up and nearly killed myself on bad torpedo juice at an off-limits party, you might have gone through life thinking you could never repay me for the little help I've given you in the unit. As it is, I think you can consider yourself paid up, Tennessee."

14

One Christmas in Petersburg

FANTASIES ARE SO ELUSIVE that many people go through life disappointed. One Christmas I caught mine, but it was like trying to hold a snowflake. When I remember those melting moments, they seem so full of magic and wonder that I think they could never have happened in the real world. Or maybe it's just the opposite. Maybe there are moments in life when the mundaneness melts away to reveal a real world where dreams come true—almost.

My dream began with a five-day Christmas pass in 1944. The commander of our tight-security unit gave us all passes as a reward for working day and night to finish the massive task of designing the terrain invasion models for Iwo Jima. We were instructed to reply only "top secret" when asked what we did; if pressured, we could say we made "visual aids." We were also to go no farther than one hundred miles from the Norfolk Naval Base.

Since home was too far away for most of us, practically everyone in the unit decided to head for Washington, D.C., where there were plenty of loose women in tight dresses and lots of honky-tonks where social drinkers usually ended up in drunken brawls. A few elected to stay in Norfolk, where there were signs that read, DOGS AND SAILORS KEEP OFF THE GRASS. I wasn't eager to spend Christmas in either place and longed to go where people did not automatically think a Navy uniform corrupts good morals. I wanted to be a *person* for a change—not a sailor with a rowdy reputation I hadn't earned.

I borrowed a map from an older man in the unit, and he suggested Petersburg, Virginia, might be a town to my liking. "There's an Army base near there but no sailors, so the mamas will be less likely to lock their daughters away when they see you coming down the street in button-front pants," he said.

I bought a bus ticket and boarded late that evening, December twenty-first. I was a very young nineteen, and as the bus rolled along in the darkness, I grew more and more excited about what might happen in Petersburg. Even though this was my first Christmas away from home and I was going to an unfamiliar place, I thought it would be a special Christmas. I had a strong feeling I would meet a lovely girl in Petersburg—someone who would make my holiday especially happy.

I stepped off the bus in Petersburg about ten o'clock that night, and the atmosphere heightened my excitement. It was a small city—about twenty thousand people—all decked out in colorful Christmas lights that winked magically while carols played from somewhere. It had not snowed yet, but the air felt right for Christmas, as if it were anticipating flakes. I walked up to a man waiting at the stoplight on the corner near the bus station and asked if there were a USO in town. He said there was and pointed to a building two blocks away.

I hurried through the cold and into the quiet USO building, surprising a little grandmotherly volunteer out of her catnap. "Oh, we have a sailor boy tonight!" she beamed, leading me over to the heater. As she warmed up the hot chocolate, she said, "We get hundreds of soldiers from Camp Lee and a Marine now and then, but we seldom get any sailors." She fussed over me while I drank the hot chocolate and told me I was ahead of the crowd; the Camp Lee crew probably wouldn't start arriving until late the next day. Then she took me upstairs and said, "You'll have your pick of the beds." It was an enormous room, like a ballroom, with about seventy beds all covered with handmade quilts. "We Petersburg ladies thought servicemen would sleep

better under quilts made by someone's mama or grandmama,"
she said proudly as she led me up to the nearest bed. "Now, you
pick out the most comfortable bed and sleep well," she said as
she left.

I tested them all until I found one that was just right. No
bears disturbed my sleep, and the next morning as I shaved, I was
still keyed up about what I would find when I went out to see
the city.

It was a cold, cloudy day and I walked briskly between the
USO and the hotel next door, crossing the alley that ran behind
the buildings. Right there on the corner was a restaurant. I
glanced in and there she was.

She was beautiful—long brown hair and hazel eyes—and
she was looking at me as she stood by the cash register just inside
the window, not four feet away from me. Neither of us actually
acknowledged the other, but our eyes were locked for just a split
second longer than the normal chance meeting of two strangers.
I couldn't believe my fantasy was coming true so quickly. I
wanted to go right in and order breakfast, but I thought that
would be too obvious—the last thing I wanted to do was look
like a typical girl-chasing sailor—so I walked two or three blocks
half-consciously looking at the town until I got up my nerve to
go back.

She was still standing at the cash register when I walked in,
and although I didn't try to meet her gaze, it seemed to me she
was watching me as I walked through the long, narrow dining
room to the last stool at the counter. I noticed she was wearing
a pretty cranberry dress with a white collar and cuffs and a bow
at the neck—very proper but not stuffy looking. When I sat
down, I turned and saw her coming toward me with a menu even
though there were two women in blue waitress uniforms standing around doing nothing.

After we exchanged "good mornings," I looked at the menu,
"I would like breakfast number two with the eggs sunny-side-
up," I said, acutely self-conscious about my Navy uniform. To
dispel any notions that I was the drunken, brawling type, I
looked her straight in the eye and said, "And I would like three

bottles of milk." I really wanted only two bottles, but I thought I should do something unusual to attract her attention.

She looked at me and said, "You want three bottles of milk?"

"That's right."

She looked at me quizzically and walked away with my order. In about ten minutes she returned with my breakfast, poured one of the bottles of milk into a glass, and said, "And here are your three bottles of milk."

She left and I ate very slowly, wondering how in the world I was going to work this into some kind of intelligent conversation. I thought about telling her we had to drink powdered milk at the base all the time, but then I thought the whole angle was pretty stupid, and she was so attractive I had to be dreaming if I thought I could ever talk with her.

I finished and took my bill to the cash register. She took the bill. We glanced at each other. I got silently angry, paid, and left. I walked all over town, through dime stores and the small department store, to hear the music, see people shopping, and smell Christmas. The store windows looked the way they're supposed to look at Christmas—it was before the advent of plastic decorations and creatures from other planets—and the carols hadn't already been played for over a month. They sounded seasonal instead of tiresome. All these trappings only made me wish for my Christmas fantasy even more, and I could not get the picture of the girl at the cash register out of my mind.

At noon I went straight back to the restaurant. I could see through the window that she was still there. I walked a block past the door and then back and in. We glanced at one another, and I went to the next to the last stool this time. When I sat down, she had already started toward me with a menu.

"Hello again," she said.

I tried to say "How are you?" distinctly as she put the menu down. Unable to abandon my lame line, I said, "I'd like a ham sandwich on plain bread and three bottles of milk."

"Three bottles?" she asked, and there was a hint of a smile behind her eyes.

"Yes, I'm on a base where we have to drink powdered milk most of the time, and I've been really thirsty for fresh milk," I said. She didn't seem impressed with my explanation.

After a while she brought the sandwich, opened one bottle of milk, and poured it into a glass, smiling a little more.

I made that sandwich last even longer than the number-two breakfast, trying to figure out as much as I could while I ate. She was back at the cash register, and once or twice I thought I saw her look at me. I thought about telling her, "Look, I need to explain to you why I'm drinking all this milk," but before I could get it worked out, two or three soldiers came in and then some more, and they all appeared to be very friendly with her. One even hugged her and said, "How are you, Sherry? I haven't seen you in so long." They were standing around the cash register, and I figured all of Camp Lee would be by pretty soon. I decided my case was hopeless and got up to pay. She gave me my change and said, "Come back and see us," smiling. I left, angry at myself, the soldiers, and the world for having to go through this.

I walked around town some more and found the Appomattox River and some Civil War monuments. I ambled into a movie theater, bought some popcorn, and watched Mrs. Minniver. I was so obsessed with my fantasy that all I could remember after the movie was Greer Garson, Walter Pidgeon, a bunch of boats and suffering, and a happy ending in spite of everything. I wandered back into the Christmas hubbub and realized I hadn't seen anyone in the whole town who was nearly as whatever as Sherry. I was sure I'd found the ideal girl, but it wouldn't do me any good if all I could do was ask her for three bottles of milk every time I saw her.

It was beginning to get dark and my healthy appetite was making itself known in spite of my misery. I told myself it would really be pointless to go back for a third meal at the same place, but I ended up walking back to look in the window from across the street. She was still there. I crossed over, went in, and passed half a dozen customers to get to my original stool at the end of the long counter. She immediately appeared with a menu. I ordered a small plate dinner. Then I looked up at her—I know I was unable to keep the desperation from pouring out of my eyes—and said, "I just want two bottles of milk."

"Just two? You're slipping tonight," she said as she wrote it down.

"Well, I've had a lot of milk today." She walked away without responding.

When she brought out my supper, it seemed to me she didn't pay as much attention to me as she had at lunch. Again I ate very slowly, trying to invent conversation. And again a group of soldiers came in and all started talking to her. I thought I saw her look at me once, but I decided I had no hope against all that competition. I sat there quietly disgusted with myself for taking that stupid milk approach and thinking of a Bible verse that had stuck in my brain years ago when Aunt Annie was reading from Job: "Thou hast poured me out like milk and curdled me like cheese." I didn't want to sit there and curdle all night, so I grabbed my bill, walked up to the cash register, and laid two dollars on the counter. She looked at me without expression as she handed me my change, and I left.

I had walked about two blocks when I looked in my hand and realized she had given me a dollar and seventy cents in change. I counted it twice. I knew my supper had to have cost more than thirty cents, so I went back to straighten it out. When I went in, there was no one there but her—or at least it seemed that way. "I believe you made a mistake," I said, holding out the change for her to see. "I only gave you two dollars."

"Oh, I guess I did make a mistake. How kind of you to come back," she said as she slowly counted the money out of my hand. There was a moment of silence. "Don't you think you could drink one more bottle of milk now that you're here?" she asked softly, smiling up at me.

"Well, I could, probably," I said tentatively, not quite believing that the milk route was getting me somewhere at last.

After what seemed to be a long pause, she said, "Why don't you go back to the back booth, and I'll bring you a glass."

"All right," I said, trying not to let myself make too much of her instructions to go to a secluded booth instead of to my usual counter stool. When she brought the milk, she also laid a roll of white cash register tape and a pen on the table. She smiled at me and went back to the cash register. On the first few inches of the roll she had written a note: "I believe I understand that we're having problems communicating. Why don't you write me what you think? I will leave here at eleven tonight and meet you in front of the USO."

Somehow I filled up both sides of the long roll of paper. I told her who I was, why I was there, and what I had hoped to find. I told her I'd been afraid I would seem too forward every time I tried to talk with her, and that I would be waiting at the USO for her at eleven. Then I walked up to pay for the milk, which I had neglected to drink, and handed her the rolled-up note and pen. She simply smiled at me and I walked out into the magic of Christmas. Back at the USO, I combed my hair six times, starting at fifteen minutes after ten. I went out and sat on the front steps at about ten-thirty just in case she got away early. By eleven twenty-five, she still hadn't come, but I was not going to give up. I had made up my mind to sit there till two in the morning if I had to.

At eleven-thirty, she walked into the hotel next door with a soldier on either arm. After about five minutes, one soldier came out and left. It was quite some time before the second one left. I waited a while longer and had finally stood up to go back inside the USO when I heard her call my name. She ran up the steps and said, "I really do apologize for this. My father is overprotective and always insists that someone in the restaurant escort me back to the hotel."

"Well, I can understand that," I said.

"Well, if you can understand my father, surely we can learn to understand each other," she said, and for the rest of our time together, "understand" was a running joke in our conversation.

"Come sit here and let me tell you why I'm staying in the hotel," she said, pulling me down on the steps.

She told me she was a sophomore at Beloit College in Wisconsin and that she had decided to come with her mother to Petersburg to spend Christmas with her father, who was a major at Camp Lee. "Since I've been here, I've been helping out in my uncle's restaurant just to keep busy," she said, "but I never expected to turn into a milk maid."

"I really didn't have to drink that much milk," I explained while she laughed. "I just suddenly became very self-conscious about my Navy uniform again and started acting a little goofy. I didn't want you to think I was trying to make a pass at you; I just wanted to talk to you and wasn't sure how to get your attention."

"I think I can understand that," she said, smiling into my eyes for a long moment. "In fact, I think it was your funny bashfulness that made me want to meet you. I'm not too fond of smooth talkers." She asked me where I was based and what I did there. When I told her I was doing top secret work at Norfolk, she nodded. "That's appropriate; it's always exciting for a chance encounter to have an element of mystery."

She wanted to know all about Memphis and life in the South, and she teased me about my slow Southern speech, while I continually had to ask her to repeat things because her words ran together so fast. I told her about my high school and tried to sound humble while I let her know I had been an undefeated runner on the school track team.

"Oh my, I suppose a track star like you has lots of young Southern belles waiting for him to come home from the war."

"I have a few girl friends back home," I said. "How about you? Is there a farm boy waiting for you in Wisconsin?"

"Well, not exactly a farm boy, and not in Wisconsin, but I *am* engaged—to a West Point man who's in Europe now." I noticed then that she was wearing a diamond ring on her left hand. "He's been in combat for over a year, but my father says the European war should be over in the next few months, and then we'll get married."

I tried not to look too deflated as she talked about the complications of being engaged to someone overseas. She told me his name, but my brain never registered it. She did say that What's-his-name was very understanding and didn't expect her to stay at home all the time, so she tried to lead a fairly normal social life. "I just don't kiss every boy I meet," she said, laughing.

"You seem to be pretty friendly with the soldiers," I said.

"Oh, they know me from my visits to Camp Lee to see Father, and they also know that he's very protective and that I'm engaged. When they start to get a little fresh, I just mention Father and they usually straighten up."

"Well, I'll be here through Christmas night," I ventured. "If you have any time, maybe we can see the city."

"I'd love to show you the city," she said. "It's really a very historical place, you know. Can you meet me at the park at two tomorrow afternoon? I promised Uncle Harry I'd work at the restaurant until then."

"I'll be there."

"Good. See you then." She ran back to the hotel and inside before I knew the conversation was ending. I stood up with some difficulty, realizing I was numb from the cold, and marveled at her diplomacy in putting our relationship on a just-friends basis. But she had made me feel we were already special friends, and I couldn't help being more excited than I needed to be.

The next day I was at the park by one-thirty; she came at two-ten. It was still cloudy, but the sun came through a little as she lectured to me about the Appomattox River and all the historical church buildings in town. We had walked about four miles before we made it back to the hotel around five o'clock. She told me she had to eat dinner with her parents (I had figured out by now that yankees said "dinner" when they really meant "supper") and asked me if I'd like to help her make some Christmas deliveries for her uncle at seven. I met her after supper, and we walked and talked for a couple of hours while she took envelopes to churches and charitable organizations.

She seemed to dominate the conversation, and I felt she was a little superior to me in intellect and especially in sophistication. We got pretty serious and philosophical, talking about the meaning of life, war, and college. We decided everybody in the world should be required to go to college and earn at least one doctorate degree. Then, by the time everyone finished going to school, no one would be young or energetic enough to fight any wars.

All of a sudden, she said, "My father would die if he knew I was with a sailor. He is extra hardheaded and dislikes the Navy. I really don't understand it; they're all fighting the same war."

"Maybe he doesn't like the Navy uniform," I suggested, not really caring what her father thought. Nothing upset me anymore. Although she was just a bit snobbish, she had a good sense of humor and was trying successfully to entertain me, always keeping the relationship in a wholesome girl-and-boy-seeing-the-city gear. I couldn't seem to help being overwhelmingly infatuated with her and the whole situation.

The next day was Christmas Eve, and she would have the whole afternoon off. We agreed to meet in the park at noon, and she ran without me up to the hotel—so her father wouldn't see—shouting back, "Pray for snow; we have to have a white Christmas!"

I was waiting for her when she came back to the park bench, on time this time. She suggested we go to a movie. I told her I'd already seen Mrs. Minniver, so we found another one. I don't remember the title or anything about this movie, because just after we sat down, she took my hand and whispered to me that What's-his-name wouldn't mind if I held her hand since it's impossible to watch a movie without holding hands. I wasn't aware of that fact, but I believed her. There I was, holding hands with a West Point man's fiancée. We held hands during the entire movie, and at least five or six times she looked over at me, saying nothing.

When we came out of the movie, it was snowing, and she was nearly ecstatic. We walked the five blocks back to the hotel, and she was like an excited child, squealing and throwing snow. I didn't immediately get all that enthralled with the cold stuff.

"Look," she said, "I promised Mother I'd help her with the Christmas preparations, but I can rush through my part and meet you in the park at eight o'clock. We can't waste this magical Christmas snow!"

"Okay," I agreed. I wouldn't be there much longer, and if I had to endure snow and bitter cold to be with her, I would.

I went back to the USO, which was full of soldiers and food, and waited upstairs on my quilted bed until seven forty-five. Then I walked back to the park. At eight-fifteen, she ran up wearing a toboggan hat, snowsuit, big coat, scarf, gloves, and galoshes. "Isn't this wonderful?" she exclaimed, pelting me with snow.

I just had a Navy peacoat over my uniform and some rubbers over my shoes and still wasn't too excited about romping in the snow. As we walked up and down the white hills, and Christmas music drifted through the flakes, and cars pulling laughing people on sleds passed us, I had to admit the snow added even more wonder to this whole fantastic situation. There's something about snow in those locations where it seldom flies that makes people want to go outside and play. Even strangers become friends, having been introduced by the elements, and defend each other when spontaneous snowball teams form. The whole town had gone that kind of crazy in the miraculous Christmas snow.

We roamed at least two miles from the hotel, but Sherry knew where she was going. We came to a park down in a valley. We looked through the surrounding chain link fence into a football stadium with a track around the field.

"You're an old track star. Do you want to go try it out?" she joked. She scrambled up and over the eight-foot-high barrier in seconds, leaving me to slip and fall back while she kidded me from the other side. When I got over, we recreated scenes from corny movies, writing our names on the snow-covered track and tackling each other between the goal posts. Finally she noticed I was freezing to death and said, "You poor thing, you're freezing. We need to rest." So she ran, leading me up the stadium steps, to a slight shelter at the base of the press box under a two-foot eave. I was so cold I was shaking as we sat and talked and joked about just talking. When we ran out of talk, I just sat and shook.

After a while she said, "I know how we can remedy your problem; I read it in a Jack London story."

"What are you talking about?"

She opened my peacoat, said, "Two bodies together create the heat of three," and pulled me against her, somehow wrapping her coat around me and mine around her. She aggressively took charge of protecting me from the cold and sort of pushed me back against the press box. We fell over into kissing that must have lasted twenty-five minutes. Nothing was said. When I remember that frozen scene of romance beneath the football press box, I always think of Kipling's line, "And we were bound up in kisses at a pagan idol's feet."

The urgency of the situation was heightened for me by the fact that I had not even seen a girl during the previous several months, but our encounter remained at least ninety percent innocent. The complications of snowsuit design and Navy buttons prevented us from doing anything that would expose very much skin to the wind and snow.

Finally we laughed and said we'd better rest for a while. After a short silence she asked, "Do you think you understand passion?"

"I think I probably do now," I answered. That led to at least fifteen more minutes of passion. Then, very suddenly, the moon came out from behind a cloud and lit the silver snow with an almost supernatural light. In another minute or two, the sky was completely clear. Just as suddenly we became serious and realized our little frolic had become a different kind of encounter. We talked with wonder about our both just happening to come to Petersburg and ending up in an empty stadium full of moonlight and snow on this magical Christmas Eve and about what kind of power was controlling all of this. She told me she had never seriously flirted with anyone since her engagement to What's-his-name and had always planned to wait for him, but now she was beginning to wonder if that was the right thing to do. We talked on and on about the future and what was important to us and what we would do if we were together. Then she looked at her watch and announced, "Regardless of what this relationship is or is not, I told my family I'd be back by midnight. It's twelve-twenty now, and it's a long walk home."

We left the feet of the pagan idol, easily scaled the fence this time, and walked rapidly over the seven little hills, which I remember distinctly for some reason, and back to town. We continued to talk all the way; she told me her whole family would be having Christmas dinner together at noon but that she would meet me in the park at two o'clock. About a block from the hotel, she turned to embrace me and said, "I'll say good night here; I know Father will be watching for me and he dislikes sailors, though I prefer them." Then she turned and ran to the hotel, leaving me alone but not sad. We had one more day together, and I felt anything could happen, judging from the events of the past two days.

The next morning, I ate doughnuts at the USO and tried to pass the time by reading the newspaper. I found it hard to concentrate even on the funny pages because I kept imagining what would happen at two o'clock in the park. Suddenly a loud female voice across the room disturbed my thoughts, saying, "You're coming with me." I looked up to see what was happening, but before I could focus my eyes, a black-haired young lady was at my elbow saying, "Where are you going to eat Christmas dinner?"

"Here, I guess," I said.

"No, you're not; you're coming with me," she said, laughing and pulling me out of my chair. "I've got mine," she yelled. The first voice I had heard yelled back, "I've got mine." I looked and saw her dragging a soldier toward the door. Another voice yelled, "I haven't got mine yet." By the time the rest of us were on the sidewalk, she had nabbed a Marine and caught up with us.

Once we were all crammed into their car, the three sisters explained that their parents had made it a holiday tradition since the war started to invite a member of each of the three branches of the armed forces for Christmas dinner. They were all loudly gregarious and joked nonstop as we rode through the sunlit snow. After about seven miles of this, I asked how far it was to their house.

"You'll find out soon enough," my escort told me. "You're so cautious! Relax a little; it's Christmas!" Then she started singing "Deck the Halls," and the others joined in almost harmony. I felt like I'd been kidnapped by the Andrews Sisters.

"Well, it's just that I have an appointment back in town at two o'clock," I interjected as soon as the noise let up some.

"Don't worry, we'll get you back in time," my escort reassured me.

About thirty minutes later, we drove up to an elegant two-story white house. When we walked in, there was a crowd of at least twenty-five people, cheering and waving flags and mistletoe. We were herded to the tree and handed presents marked "To the Sailor," "To the Soldier," and "To the Marine." Then we went to the dining room and sat down to huge mounds of food. While we ate, the girls' father asked each of us what we were doing in the war. The soldier and the Marine both told how many men they'd shot in battle, and I said, "I can't tell what I do."

"Why not?" the black-haired girl asked.

"Security," I answered.

"Oh," she said and turned to hear more from the other two.

After dinner, we had to participate in games and songs. I mentioned my appointment again to the black-haired girl a little before two and she said, "Just a little longer; we'll make it back in time."

At last, she took the soldier and me back to town—the Marine decided to stay and be the main attraction for supper. It was four-thirty when I jumped out of the car and sprinted across the street to the park. No one was there. I sat on the bench for nearly an hour. It was dark when the clerk from the hotel walked over and asked if I were Al. He handed me a note from Sherry.

She had written, "I went to the park at two and waited for fifty minutes, but you never came. The roads cleared up and my family wanted to leave at three for Washington, D.C., to visit some other relatives. I so had hoped you would come; I had something special to tell you. Be careful in the war with your secret mission, whatever it is. Perhaps we will meet again somewhere in the world, but perhaps not. Affectionately, Sherry."

I sat for a while on the back of the bench and then went to the USO and got some free food before catching the bus to Norfolk. As I rode along in the darkness, it seemed I was slowly waking up from a wonderful dream and having trouble figuring out what was in the dream and what was not.

I walked into the barracks about midnight and was greeted by some of the brawlers who had just returned from Washington. They kidded me about my big weekend in Petersburg and asked if I saw any action there. I started to tell them but I stopped, knowing they wouldn't believe it or understand it, as innocent as it all was.

After the war, I often thought about trying to find Sherry, but I never did. Lately I've realized that without the Christmas lights and drifting flakes and wafting music and my anticipation that something special was going to happen, the magic would most likely be gone. I prefer to leave the fantasy untarnished, like those memories of childhood Christmases before wiser people told me Santa Claus wasn't real.

15

Luther's Tea

IN FEBRUARY, 1945, OUR terrain invasion model unit left
Norfolk on a cargo ship that was taking a shipment of small
boats and beer to the Philippines, but none of us knew where
we'd end up. It was rumored we were going to Pearl Harbor.

We picked up a destroyer escort as we passed through the
Panama Canal, and for three days we headed straight out into
the Pacific. Then, for some reason, our escort turned right and
disappeared, leaving us to fend for ourselves. The captain's voice
announced: "Now hear this, now hear this. We've lost our
destroyer escort and have detected an enemy sub in the area, so
we will be zigzagging to avoid being an easy target."

We headed toward the equator—in an effort, I supposed, to
confuse the sub. None of the one hundred eighty men in our unit
had ever crossed the equator. We were fearful we'd have to go
through the Navy's traditional ceremony in which "polliwogs"
become "shellbacks" in the society of *Neptunus Rex.* We
believed the ritual entailed being whipped with hoses. The
regular crew didn't like us being leisurely passengers while they
worked, and we figured they'd have enjoyed the opportunity to
rough us up a little.

Before the destroyer's desertion, we had been sleeping down
in the ship's hold with the beer. Now that we were in a more
precarious situation, we were given permission to sleep on the

top deck so we'd have a better chance of survival if we were torpedoed. We were also instructed to keep our eyes peeled for periscopes. There was not much to do except to be bored or terrified or to complain about the heat and lack of fresh water and ice. Even getting a suntan wouldn't do to pass the time, since we were already browned beyond recognition. We could take showers—and many in our unit were inclined to do so after gazing for hours at photographs of pin-up girls—but only with salt water, which left the skin feeling sticky and itchy. We ate two meals a day—one early in the morning and one at four in the afternoon. Our added numbers had put a severe strain on the supplies of the ship, which normally carried only its crew of thirty-five men.

It finally got to the point that we mainly just sat around and talked about how good a glass of iced tea would taste or how much we'd give for just one cold Coke. "One cold Coke would only make you miss what you don't have even more," my buddy Paloff said, "but we may be in for a tantalizing treat this afternoon: I've heard rumors the officers are going to surprise us by sharing their ice and tea with everybody for late chow."

The rumor was all over the ship before noon. Even if there were nothing to it, at least it gave us something to anticipate and speculate about for most of the day. Midafternoon, Paloff said to me, "Why don't you come with me? I know a secret place where we can look into the galley and see if they're really making tea." I went with him down several dark passages and ladders. Halfway down the last ladder, he showed me a slot through which we could look into the galley. We peered in from our perch to find, in order of rank and height, the galley's chief petty officer, a first-class cook, and a diminutive third-class-seaman cook whom we all knew as Luther.

The chief petty officer—about six feet two, built like a fullback, and loudly verbose—was shouting profanities at both the other men, telling them to "get on this iced tea; we're behind!" He stormed out, leaving the first class cook to scream at his inferior.

"You heard what he said, you puny little makeshift excuse for a human being! Get it ready!" the cook blasted at Luther, and then let out a string of irreverent exhortations and obscene aspersions on Luther's manhood and intelligence. I never got used to the language I heard in the Navy, and my reaction to it alternated between total block-out and wide-eared wonder at the creativity evident in the combinations of words and phrases I had seldom, if *ever* heard before. I used to wonder how many more literary geniuses the world would've had if the more inventively cursing sailors had bent their talent from profanity to poetry or prose.

When Luther was left alone, he stood there looking at the enormous aluminum vat full of tea. He was still staring stupidly at the vat, which was four feet wide and three feet deep, when the cook came back in and said, "What the hell are you just standing there for?"

"What should I do?" Luther asked helplessly.

"Get the sugar in it, idiot," the cook shouted, and with more profanities he stomped back out.

So Luther dragged out several large sacks of sugar while Paloff and I watched and wondered how much he could add, the tea being only a few inches from the rim of the vat. He had just finished pouring the sugar in when the cook returned and called him everything in the world that was foul and unintelligent. "What are you still standing there for?" he demanded before disappearing again. "Stir it up!"

Luther found a huge paddle and started to stir. Then the chief petty officer returned and yelled, "You are so *slow;* get the ice." More profanity.

The ice came in slabs about twelve inches long, six inches wide, and one inch thick. Luther brought them out from the officers' provisions and put them in the tea. They floated around on top like little barges. The chief petty officer was watching and said, "You have to break the ice up, you idiot." He punctuated his disbelief at Luther's ineptness with another string of expletives.

The cook chimed in, "That's right; break it up." He cut loose with a barrage of demeaning oaths and abusive slander that seemed to shock even the chief petty officer—at least, he stopped swearing to listen to the cook curse for a while. They left for a few minutes and Luther used the paddle to break up the ice, sloshing some of the precious tea over the rim. The cook and the chief both came back in and told him to keep stirring the tea, reminding him again that he had subhuman intelligence.

When they left, Luther seemed engrossed in digging the sugar up from the bottom of the vat and stirring the tea in a circular motion. Soon he stopped digging up the sugar and was concerned only with making the chunks of ice on top float around in the wake of his paddle. Then, dreamily, he heisted his greasy, grimy foot and let it ride, tennis shoe and all, in the circular motion with the ice. He discarded his paddle, looked around to be sure he was alone, lowered his whole leg into the vat, and stirred with vengeance.

Luther had enough sense to cut his fun short before his superiors came back in to check on him. He had just pulled out his leg and was letting it drip dry when they came in and cursed him some more. He only smiled at them.

As Paloff and I dragged ourselves back up to the top deck, I said, "I don't think I'm going to drink any iced tea at chow tonight, are you?"

"No," he said.

But we agreed not to tell the rest of the parched sailors; we didn't want to spoil their treat, and it probably wouldn't kill them, we decided. We went in to chow, and there was little Luther, standing at the end of the serving line and pouring tea with a big smile. Everyone but Paloff and me raved about the tea. I got some ice out of my glass, washed it off, and made ice water. I watched Luther, pouring and smiling away, graciously offering seconds until the tea was all gone.

About a week later, a few days before we were put ashore at Pearl, we were again surprised at late chow with iced tea. When I got to the end of the line, little Luther was pouring, and I declined my ration. I didn't trust that smile.

We got close to but never crossed the equator on that voyage. Seems to me Luther's tea might have been at least as hazardous as induction into the ranks of shellbacks.

16

Granger

GRANGER LOOKED LIKE ERROL Flynn and was undoubtedly the most sophisticated sailor in our Navy unit. He was thirty-two and would probably never look any older. He was tall and slender—but strong, not willowy. Black wavy hair set off his steely eyes and almost too-pretty teeth ever showing through his smile. It was hard to imagine him tied down to the wife and two children who were waiting for him in his native Boston.

Granger was more than just a fine physical specimen. Having studied at Dartmouth, he considered himself an intellectual and was forever reminding us of the superiority of the Eastern intellect and culture. I looked up to him as a model of the sophisticated life and felt honored to be included in his discussions occasionally. I was just a green kid from Memphis, and thought that with Granger's help I was learning to get along anywhere in the world.

When the war ended, I got officially lost. We were shipped back from Hawaii to the mainland, and I was ordered to Nashville to pick up my reassignment papers. I was told that there were no records of my service. I stayed at the local YMCA while the Navy tried to find my papers. After two weeks, they told me that I was a lost service person and sent me to the Navy's island of lost souls, Shoemaker Naval Camp, out from Oakland, California.

Shoemaker was an appropriately barren and bleak place. I arrived there in November, 1945, and immediately sank into an uncharacteristic depression thinking about the futility of being lost in the Navy. I was shuffling down the street, wondering what would become of me, when I happened to look up and see Granger's undaunted face. Surely Granger could help get us out of here. If not, he would at least prevent my becoming a mental vegetable.

We were assigned to the same barracks and were both put on spud locker duty. We worked alternate shifts—one day on and one day off—preparing fourteen vats of potatoes for cooking, which took about three hours. We'd usually run into each other for a visit before I left the base for my twenty-four-hour leave.

One day soon after we had gotten into our potato routine, Granger came by with a letter from some relatives that he didn't even know he had in Oakland. They had invited him to their home for dinner. He was understandably excited because these cousins were formerly from Boston and would no doubt provide him with a stimulating evening.

The next time we talked, Granger was eager to tell me about his visit with his newly-found kinfolks. "Al, let me tell you something," he began. "My relatives in Oakland have a wonderful, tasteful home. He's a publisher and they're very active in cultural affairs. They understand the world and knew it would be wrong to sit all evening and talk just about family, so they invited a beautiful, intelligent young woman from San Francisco to dine with us and to balance out our group. We had very enlightening conversation. It was really so thoughtful of them to invite her because her husband is stationed in Alaska; naturally, she's lonely and needs company."

My face must have betrayed my astonishment at his cousins' throwing two married people together in what sounded like a double date. He replied to my look, "This is just the way Boston people perceive the world, Al. There is nothing to be read into the fact that Ovita is a lovely lady; she was just needed to balance the group and add another perspective to our discussion."

"Why didn't they invite a man, then?" I asked—logically, I thought.

"Because it is proper to have two men and two women for a social evening," he explained patiently. Granger sometimes gave the impression that it was his mission to enlighten me to Bostonian thought; my lack of sophistication rarely angered him.

Toward the end of November, Christmas music was starting to show up in concert programs. I went to a performance of Handel's "Messiah" to celebrate my twentieth birthday, and Granger was invited to dinner with his cousins and Ovita again.

"Isn't it marvelous?" We were drinking a Coke in the PX after this second experience. "I can't get over how people can understand the world as much as they do. We had wonderful conversation, and afterwards Ovita drove me to the base. She has a beautiful roadster."

I must have had that look again.

"Tomorrow I'll give you a talk on *philos, eros,* and *agape,*" he said. "You have a lot to learn."

"Why, I haven't said a thing," I said, trying to cover up my gut feeling that Granger was getting more than an intellectual buzz on his evenings out.

"This relationship between me and Ovita is strictly *philos*—mutual warmth and intellectual stimulation between two socially compatible people," he explained.

I felt pretty naive as he walked sharply away to peel potatoes.

Several days passed and Granger told me, "Ovita has invited me to go to San Francisco to the opera."

"Are your cousins going, too?" I asked.

"Al, you have so much to learn. Of course they are not going. They don't have to chaperone us. We are no more than two people who understand each other intellectually."

So Granger and Ovita went to the opera.

Afterwards, back at the PX, Granger tried to teach me about relationships among the enlightened. "Let me tell you how this works," he said. "This is all very wholesome. I got off the train.

Ovita met me. We had a wonderful dinner, went to the opera, and walked to her home, where we stood out front for a while discussing the performance. I kissed her on the cheek—nothing sexual—we shook hands, and I left. This is the real world, Al. When you get older, you'll understand. This is what we call *philos* in Boston."

"Well, I've never heard of *philos,* but I'm learning," I said.

By early December, I was getting more and more anxious about my lost condition. I had heard that sailors whose records were never found were shipped to Hiroshima to help clean up. I checked the bulletin board daily to see if my records and orders had come in, but I was always disappointed. Granger checked too, but he never seemed too concerned. He was always more interested in discussing his plans for the next intellectual rendezvous with Ovita and what had happened during the previous one.

On one occasion, he told me, she had shown him a photo of her husband. "This," he said, "just reinforces the fact that we are two super intellectual souls enjoying a philotic relationship, which does nothing to hinder the relationships we have with our spouses."

His next meeting with Ovita was at a play in San Francisco. Afterwards at the PX, he gave me further insight into intellectual socializing.

"When we left the play," he said, "Ovita invited me to her apartment—in the most beautiful part of town—for a drink. We talked until two in the morning about religion, philosophy, and various people that we admire. She walked with me to the street; then she pulled me down and kissed me gently on the lips."

"But I didn't think you touched each other like that in a philotic relationship," I said, confused.

"It's okay as long as you understand that it's simply philotic," he explained. I didn't understand.

A few days later, Granger went in to town for a movie and an intellectual conversation with Ovita. The next morning around eleven o'clock, he passed me in the barracks and had nothing to say.

I was ready for our next session in this complicated course and said, "Hey, Granger, you wanna go get a Coke?"

"I have some things to do, Al."

I couldn't believe it. This was the first time he had not wanted to talk about philos.

"What's wrong?"

"I really have nothing to say, Al. And I have some letters to get off this morning."

In silence, we passed by the bulletin board. We looked at it and saw orders posted for Granger to leave that night at eight o'clock for the East coast. This meant he was immediately frozen to the base until the train would haul him away.

I slapped him on the back and shouted, "Congratulations, Granger, you're found!"

"Al, have you got any money?" he asked, rather agitated.

"Only ten dollars."

"I'm broke. Would you let me have five? I'll pay you back. I've got to get in touch with Ovita."

I gave him the money, and he tried to call her at once but couldn't get her. All day long, he packed and called. By seven o'clock, he still hadn't gotten her. He fidgeted while I helped get the last of his things together.

Just before the train left, he said, "Look, you've got to do me the greatest favor in the world. I have here a letter you must get to Ovita in person. Under no circumstances should you mail it. Put it in her hands, and I will be forever indebted. If you can't get it to her, tear it up."

"I'll get it to her, Granger," I promised as the train pulled out.

The next day, I took my last five dollars and left for San Francisco about two in the afternoon. I arrived toward sunset and went to the address Granger had given me. An elderly woman came to the door and told me Ovita was working late and would probably get home about seven o'clock.

Granger was right; it was sure enough a picturesque place. Trolleys clanged musically up and down the well-kept hills dotted with light stone buildings. Everything was neat and clean, punctuated with sharp afternoon shadows.

I got something to eat and came back to put myself on the steps so I could observe. By seven o'clock, Ovita still hadn't arrived. I started walking around when my legs began to go to sleep, but I stayed close to the building and never took my eyes off the front door for more than a few seconds.

About nine o'clock, the roadster Granger had described drove up and parked in front of the apartment building. A soldier and a tall, beautiful woman with blondish hair got out. I heard him call her Ovita as they laughed and chatted on their way into the building.

I decided to wait until the soldier left before I went up to deliver the mysterious letter, so I put myself back on the steps. At eleven-thirty, I gave up on that idea and left for the base with plans to return in two days.

The next morning, on my way to the spud locker, I glanced at the bulletin board and saw my reassignment orders for the Photographic Intelligence Center in Washington, D.C. Now I was frozen to the base until the train was to leave at eight o'clock that night. My brain forsook all other thoughts as it filled with the sheer elation of leaving Shoemaker.

That night I slept sitting up on the train. I woke the next morning to a fairyland outside the window as the train pulled through the Sierra Nevadas on the Great Feather Route. Suddenly I remembered that Granger's letter to Ovita was among my papers. I took it out and held it for a long time. I knew I had to tear it up, but he hadn't told me exactly how I should do it. I began by tearing the envelope. Then I removed the twelve-page message and read it. I watched the scenery for a while and then slowly read the letter a second time before tearing it into hundreds of pieces. Granger was right; I had an awful lot to learn.

I never heard from Granger again. He still owes me five dollars.

17

Daddy's Girl

ALMOST EVERY MAN WHO came home from World War II has a hitchhiking story; I'm no different.

When I was discharged from the Navy in 1946 at the age of twenty, I struck out across the country visiting colleges and universities to see which one best suited me. I ruled out Alfred University in New York solely on the basis of the weather—it was forty-five degrees there one morning in July—and decided to head back home to Memphis. I didn't have much in my pockets but my thumbs, so I put them to work.

By the time I made it to Louisville, Kentucky, I had learned that wearing a coat and tie is a boon to hitching. So Louisville saw me up early and suited to the chin, hoping to impress someone with my respectability before the Southern sun started to stew me in my own juices.

I had been standing on the outskirts of town for about an hour and a half when an old but very fancy green Packard drove by slowly enough that I could see an attractive young woman at the wheel. She turned right two blocks down the street and in a couple of minutes pulled up beside me. As she leaned across to roll down the passenger window and ask where I was going, I could see that she was more attractive than she needed to be. I had to break my usual habit of understatement and admit to myself that she was really a bombshell—any red-blooded American serviceman's ideal.

I told her I was going to Memphis and tried not to stare at the areas of her body her red two-piece bathing suit did and did not cover. A two-piecer was about the most revealing outfit girls could wear then, and they never wore them if they weren't in or near the water. I couldn't help but be a little embarrassed, as if I'd walked in on someone in her underwear.

"I can carry you as far as Nashville," she said, tossing her long, thick strawberry blond hair behind her. "Put your bag in the back seat and jump in." She spoke matter-of-factly, but the words dripped from her Southern tongue like bacon grease, and I felt a little more at ease.

When I opened the back door, I saw the whole back of the car was full of a loose assortment of china cups, silverware, huge silver teapots and serving pieces, and a pile of men's and women's clothes—but no baggage.

"Don't worry about all of that," she said impatiently. "Just put your bag on top and hop in."

As soon as I did, the car started jumping. "I've done something to the gears; it'll quit after we get going good," she explained and flashed an apologetic smile at me. "My name's Roberta. What's yours?"

"Al," I said, looking straight ahead to avoid staring at her.

She drove pretty fast—but it probably seemed faster than it actually was because her steering was jerky and felt unsafe. After we'd gone about ten miles, she said, "I must tell you the truth of what's going on here. I am running away from my husband, and it's more than likely that he or someone from his bank is after me. This is the second time I've tried to go back to my daddy in Knoxville; he won't let me leave. I just struck out in the middle of the night and I'm taking this long way around. He wouldn't expect me to come this way, so maybe I'll make it home before he catches me.

"I'm telling you this because it would be unfair not to let you know what you've gotten into, and I'll let you out right now if you want me to. Bruce is a very jealous man, but if he or one of his men catches us, I'll explain you're just a hitchhiker I picked up because I needed someone to talk to me and keep me awake. We should make it to Nashville late this afternoon."

My conservative side told me to get out of the car quick, but it was getting pretty hot outside, and I didn't want to stand out on the highway in a coat and tie for another hour and a half. I also would have felt bad if I had deserted this forthright bombshell, who might go to sleep at the wheel and crash without me. I told her I'd stay with her to Nashville.

For the next twenty minutes, she didn't talk but kept checking the rearview mirror. Finally she said, "I don't think they would believe I'd go this way, but if you don't mind, look back occasionally, and if anyone appears to be following, let me know."

Of course, it seemed to me that every car I saw behind was following us—I'd seen too many James Cagney movies—but we rolled up and over the Kentucky hills with no encounters. Every time we went through a small town, she would slow down to fifteen or twenty miles per hour, and the car would buck for about seven blocks until we finally would jump back into road speed. She suggested it might be better if I drove but quickly dismissed that because it would be hard to explain if we were caught.

I continued to look straight ahead and straight behind as she talked about her life. She had attended the University of Tennessee in Knoxville, where her family made lots of money in investments. When she was twenty-two and about to finish her degree, she fell in love with Bruce, an older man (in his thirties) who was visiting her father about business. They got married and she went to live with him in his big house in Cincinnati, where he was vice president of a bank. It was the typical story. He was rich and busy; she was miserable and neglected.

"I called Daddy all the time just to talk to someone who really cared about me," she said. "Finally, Daddy asked me, 'Why don't you just come on home?' but Bruce wouldn't hear of it."

We drove on, looking back all the time. I grew more and more suspicious about the stuff in the back seat and started imagining all kinds of things. I could almost feel the machine gun bullets.

She kept saying how hot and tired she was. "You may think it's funny that I'm wearing my bathing suit," she said, totally unembarrassed, "but I knew it would be hot and decided to try to be as cool as possible."

I have pretty fair peripheral vision, and as I looked straight ahead, I could see her stretching out her halter top to let air sift through her bosom. She talked a lot and seemed very self-confident and in control in spite of her precarious situation.

"I've got to stop and eat; I'm starved," she announced. "I haven't had any food since yesterday." We found a small restaurant about eleven o'clock. As she pulled in, I suggested that she back up onto the slope in the parking area so she could get momentum and avoid so many jerks when we started again. She said I was brilliant for thinking of that and then asked if I would run in and see if it would be okay for her to come in as she was dressed.

I went in and saw only one customer at the long counter. I asked a big man standing at the grill if a lady in a bathing suit could come in, and he said, "As long as she's not wet."

I went back out to get her. As she picked her way slowly through the gravel, somewhat handicapped by her high heels, I noticed again how unusually well put-together she was. Without seeming to vamp, she oozed sensuality as she brushed her long hair and swung her hips to just the right degree. As we took a booth, the cook, the waitress, and the customer were visibly struck by her presence also. People just did not see women clad this skimpily in public in 1946, and Roberta did a lot for skimpy clothes.

We sat down and ordered sandwiches and Cokes. I was mentally figuring how much money I'd have left after paying for my lunch when she looked directly at me and said, "You're sort of a shy type of fellow, aren't you?"

"I suppose so," I admitted. "I've been told that, but I've known people who are quieter than I am."

"You're sensitive and shy," she added.

"Well, I am sensitive," I agreed. I told her about being drafted into the Navy, being self-conscious of the reputation sailors had, looking for a place to study art, and hitchhiking because I only had three dollars and twenty-five cents.

"Don't worry, I'll take care of the meal," she said when I mentioned my finances. "It's worth that much to have you with me to keep me awake." She held her cigarette in a classic pose and blew vertical smoke. Then she got up and swayed to the door to look out, drawing all eyes to her again.

She came back to pick up the check and opened a large, long, deep cloth bag with a wooden top. Near the top were at least seven bundles of banded money, from which she pulled a twenty-dollar bill. After she paid, I offered to drive, anticipating more jumps and jerks if she were at the wheel, but she insisted that it would put us both in more danger should we be caught. "You just keep me awake," she instructed. So I coached her down the hill, and she did pretty well. I continued to suspect every car that passed us and wasn't digesting my lunch very well. About fifteen minutes later, we came to a little town with a courthouse and diagonal parking around the square. She parked on the square and sent me to the dime store across the street with two dollars to buy her a bandana. "My hair is just too hot; I've got to tie it up," she explained.

"Any color bandana?" I asked.

"Just something that will go with my hair."

I was very careful to get a tasteful bandana for the bombshell, choosing a bluish-gray one with a white design. When I came back out, the car was gone and I panicked, thinking of my discharge papers and my bag that held everything I owned. I started running like a wild chicken across the courtyard to find the police. Then I heard her honk and saw her driving around the block, ready to go.

"Where in the world were you going?" she asked.

"To find a drink of water," I said, jumping in the car. We lurched out of the town while everyone on the sidewalks watched.

She took out the bandana and tried to tie up her hair with one hand and steer with the other. Finally she asked me, "Would you steer for me while I fix this, please?"

I had to sit very close to her, touching her hot body with my arm. All the while she was looking back and telling me to keep an eye out.

"You know, I still don't know if Bruce would understand your being here," she said, almost to herself.

"I thought you were going to tell him I'm just a hitchhiker," I said with some added concern.

"But he has such a strange mind," she mused.

"Just talk fast and tell him I'm on my way to Memphis, trying to find a college." It sounded pretty weak to me, too.

I looked back and saw a bluish car. "That car has been about a quarter of a mile behind us for quite a while now," I said after a few minutes.

She looked and didn't say anything. After a while I checked again and said, "That car is still back there."

"I'll slow down and see what happens," she said. For a while the bluish car lagged behind. She seemed pretty cool-headed while I was imagining flying bullets and all sorts of drama. Finally the car zoomed past us and went over the hill.

For a while no one was behind us. Suddenly she said, "Wouldn't it be wonderful if we could go for a swim?"

"I guess so," I said. I hadn't really thought about it.

She stopped and asked an old farmer if he knew of a swimming hole anywhere close by. He said he didn't, but I figured he just wasn't interested in talking very long with a brazen girl wearing a bathing suit and smoking a cigarette. So we bucked back onto the road.

"Good Lord, if I could just swim for ten or fifteen minutes, I could wake up!" she said in exasperation. "Maybe I need to take a nap. If I took a nap and a shower, I could drive on to Knoxville tonight. That's what I'll do."

I didn't say anything, but I could envision Bruce busting into a tourist court room and choking me to death even though I had all my clothes on.

We passed a few cabins with "no vacancy" signs, and she started to curse. I looked back and saw the same blue car and told her. "It does look like the same car," she said, continuing to look for a tourist court.

Finally she pulled off onto a gravel drive where a motel was under construction. "Run in there and see if there are any rooms available yet," she said as the blue car drove past and the driver glanced over at us.

I went in and asked, "How far is it to Nashville?"

"About forty miles," the woman at the desk told me.

I ran out and jumped back in the car. "The lady in there said Nashville is only forty miles away, and there are a lot of good hotels there," I said. I knew I couldn't flat lie to her. She looked at me suspiciously and bucked back on the road.

We were both very quiet all the way to Nashville, where she stopped at a sign that said "Memphis—79 Highway."

"I turn off toward Knoxville from here," she said. "I guess you want out. I hope you make it in to Memphis okay."

"You need to stop and rest," I told her. "You'll never make it if you don't rest."

"I'll make it some way," she said. She smiled at me as I closed the door, and then she bucked back into the traffic. As she disappeared down the highway, I saw the same blue car about a half a block behind her.

18

The Hooter

LOUISIANA STATE UNIVERSITY turned out to be the college I was looking for. During my first year there, I lived at the Pentagon Barracks Athletic Dormitory in the C-5 section, where they put athletes in the minor sports and last string football players. I was a delicate runner, weighing about one hundred fifty-eight pounds at six-two. My roommates were two piles of dead weight on the football team named Mather and Ashlock; each weighed about two-fifty, had very little brain power, and qualified as an advanced thug.

Mather and Ashlock knew they were bad athletes, but this only made them more hostile and belligerent. It seemed their favorite occupation was trying to take brute advantage of me and the other skinny guys in golf, tennis, and track.

One Saturday, after about three months of this harassment, I was down at the Tiger Town Drugstore and saw a box of hooters—big pull whistles made from spinners on double strings. I pulled one out and set it spinning, unable to keep a shiver from going down my spine as it made its wonderfully eerie, whirring noise. It occurred to me that one of these could cause old Mather and Ashlock some discomfort in spite of their brute force, so I paid a quarter for one, took it back to the dorm, and put it under the mattress on the bottom bunk bed where I slept. No one slept above me; the two thugs slept in bunks about eight feet across from mine against the opposite wall.

That night, they finally went to sleep about an hour and a half after the lights went out. I roused myself from my own half-sleep and reached under my mattress for the hooter. I had cleverly thrown my towel on the side of the top bunk to dry after I had showered so that my head and arms would be hidden in case the moon lit up the room or someone suddenly flipped on the light. As I lay in the dark, I started pulling the hooter and let it emit its wild call one time. In a little while, I heard Mather say, "Ashlock!"

"Yeah."

"Did you hear somethin'—sounded kinda like some kind of animal?"

I waited about ten minutes and started pulling again until they began to talk nervously about it again. Then I crammed the hooter back under the mattress and went to sleep.

The next morning at breakfast, Mather told everybody at the training table about the strange noise they'd heard. It just so happened that the spring of 1947 had been about the wettest season ever around Baton Rouge; there was water all over campus and the Mississippi was about to overflow. Someone at the table suggested that Mather's phantom noisemaker might be some creature that had been washed up by the floods. By that afternoon, everyone on campus had heard that some strange new animal had washed up in the Pentagon Barracks Dorm. It was an explanation that seemed to hold water; a lake had formed behind the Barracks and was almost up to the rear wall.

That night I pulled out the hooter about one-thirty and whirred it again behind my towel. Mather started getting antsy, and I thought I'd give it one more whirr for good measure. Just as I did, Mather jumped off his top bunk, shaking the floor as he landed. I jammed the hooter under my mattress and pretended to be sound asleep before his eyes had time to stop shaking from the jolt. He turned on the lights and made me and Ashlock get up and search the lockers and poke behind the radiators and under the bunks. On the third night, Mather suspected that I was making the sound some way with my mouth and told me to talk while the noise was in progress. So I talked aloud about what in the world could be making that noise while I whirred the hooter in the darkness of my bunk; it seemed to convince him of my innocence.

Breakfast talk was wild the next morning. People in several rooms in C-5 had heard the noise, which was most likely made by some kind of bayou or swamp animal that could probably crawl up walls, they said. This went on for about a week and with very little effort on my part. I was careful not to overdo it; a little hooting went a long way through the vents in the Barracks. One night I made it whirr only once, went back to sleep, and let them suffer.

During that week, LSU's school paper, *The Daily Reveille,* ran a story about the reported sounds of strange animals on campus and a recent sighting of an alligator behind Pentagon Barracks. Of course, it didn't take long for these stories to merge, and soon the young kids from farther north could be heard asking, "Can alligators crawl up brick walls?"

One night about one o'clock, I took out my hooter to give all the creature-hunters what they were waiting for. I was in the middle of a nice eerie whirr when suddenly I was pounced upon. Within a moment, Mather and Ashlock had given me a pretty good wringing out. Mather had me by the throat and was ready to deliver the grand finale punch when I croaked out, barely audible, "No one knows but us."

Mather gazed at me two seconds while his slobber dribbled on my face. "What do you mean?" he asked—one of his more articulate utterances because he practiced it a lot in everyday life.

"I mean, no one else knows what's making the noise. Let's keep it going."

He looked a little confused and threw me back down on the bunk. "We'll talk about it tomorrow," he grunted, and he and Ashlock lumbered back to bed. He threatened to beat me up again before breakfast, but the renewed swamp monster talk at the chow hall changed his mind. Soon he and Ashlock were co-conspirators with me, and my hide was spared for a while longer.

That night, Ashlock told me and Mather that he'd heard Joe Wayne Haney had not slept in three nights because of the noise. Joe Wayne was a freshman football player who'd been brought from his father's farm in north Louisiana on scholarship. He was on academic probation because he hated school and didn't know what to do in class. The coaches had a squad of tutors working with him to get his grade average up enough to play next fall. He had a nineteen-inch neck and a solid body of proportionate dimensions, about six foot three. I'd heard that he could pick up a linebacker and pitch him like a bale of hay, but he had an unassuming and almost gentle disposition. All he wanted to do was go home and feed the cattle. There were just too many people in Baton Rouge for him to be comfortable.

The baseball players who were Joe Wayne's roommates had told Ashlock he had begged them to keep the light on when the strange sounds first started the week before. Of course, they wouldn't turn on the light and probably enjoyed seeing the big guy suffer. This information inspired Mather to go to greater lengths in bringing the creature to life that night. He ordered me to spin the hooter while he leaned out the window, as Ashlock held on to his thighs, and scratched Joe Wayne's window with a broom. It sounded horrible. Suddenly all three roommates next door were out in the hallway. "That damn thing was on my windowsill!" Joe Wayne almost screamed. We all ran out and said, "We heard it, too."

The next morning, I got up at seven and went to shave in the big bathroom that everyone in C-5 shared. I was usually the first one there, but that morning, Joe Wayne was asleep on the floor with all the lights on.

When Mather got out the hooter again that night, I said I thought we should retire the creature.

"What do you mean?" Mather asked. He was almost ignorant enough to be innocent.

"Quit it—you know—stop doing it."

"What for? Nobody suspects us."

"I know, but I'm starting to feel bad about this; people are losing sleep. Besides, this animal has been squawking for ten days; surely it's time for it to migrate."

"I think he's turning into a sister on us, Mather," Ashlock smirked.

"Yeah, well he didn't have far to go, and he knows what'll happen to him if he says anything now, dontcha, pansy?" With that he started pulling the whistle, making it sound more and more vicious. Soon we heard mass bumbling and practically everyone on the whole third floor piled out into the hall. It was Mather's finest hour.

The next day as I walked from class, I saw Joe Wayne standing behind the Barracks and looking out over the flooded area that supposedly spawned our swamp creature. He cast a hulking shadow over the water, but his face was sad and sweet and reminded me of the big, beautiful, drooping faces of the Brahman bulls that seem to languish in stalls at the state fair. I suddenly felt much older than this farm boy and guilty for having bothered him so. I approached him from the side so as not to startle him and said, "Joe Wayne, I want to talk to you a little bit." He just looked at me.

I plowed ahead and told him the whole story of buying the hooter at the Tiger Town Drugstore so I could torment my roommates. "It's just a practical joke that got out of hand, Joe Wayne. There are no animals that crawl up the walls or alligators that washed up in the Barracks. I'm sorry I started the whole mess."

He continued to look at me with no change of expression. "You don't have to make up a story to make me feel better," he said.

I couldn't convince him I was telling the truth. That night, Joe Wayne snuck out, headed home, and never came back. I got with Mather and Ashlock and said, "Look, you know what's happening all over campus, and now one of our potential All-Americans has left because of this stupid hooter. Don't you think it's about time we get rid of it? The coaches aren't going to take this lightly, and sooner or later they'll get to the bottom of what's scaring their athletes away. We can't go on forever. Even Pretty Boy Floyd finally got caught."

That must have gotten to them. On the way to supper that night, Ashlock threw the hooter into the encroaching water behind the Barracks. It took a while for the rumors to die down; people kept hearing strange noises in the night for at least a week after the whistle drowned.

A few years later, Joe Wayne's little brother came to LSU and ended up as an All-American. Joe Wayne never even left the farm to come watch him play.

19

My First Analysis

MY THREE BEST FRIENDS at Louisiana State University were Dan, Kent, and Gardner. All three were athletes in the minor sports, so we lived in the same dorm, and all three majored in psychology. Though I was an art major, I took all my electives in psychology. This was in the late forties when the discipline was just beginning its popularity on college campuses, and there was an extra pride among its students, who were held in somewhat unusual regard.

The Field House was LSU's social center, and in it was a special corner where psychology majors and minors hung out. No one else went there, but sometimes my three friends would allow me to wander in with them and join the talk about psyches and Freud.

One day I was there with Dan when a graduate student dropped by the corner and told the group that LSU's first graduate seminar in psychology would spend a semester studying art students on campus. Starting the next Tuesday afternoon, the graduate students would go to one of the studios, which were all open to the public, to try to analyze the artists by looking at their work and observing their eccentric ways.

The graduate student who told us this news didn't know an art student was in the group, and Dan wasn't aware I was even listening to the conversation. He would have never suspected that I might divulge this academic secret, anyway. Of course, I never told a soul about what the sneaky psychology students planned to do, but the next Sunday afternoon, as I was working on an assignment in the painting studio, I got the idea to do a special painting for our unannounced student analysts. I got out a large canvas board and some fast-drying casein paint and started a painting of a wall. A scantily clad female figure was chained to the wall, and crawling toward her were all manner of snakes, lizards, spiders, and creeping things. I even invented some new varmints for added horror. I finished it Sunday evening.

On Tuesday afternoon, I put away my real work and got the "Woman with Varmints" back out and set it on my easel in the studio. There were about fifty easels set up, all facing the walls of the studio, and the student artists were sitting on stools, working with their backs to the windows so that visitors could stroll around and view their work without disturbing them.

About midafternoon, twelve serious people gathered outside the door and then nonchalantly walked in one or two at a time as if they were not part of a conspiracy. As I pretended to put some final casein touches on my painting, I decided to twitch my left shoulder occasionally, and instead of stepping back to view my work, I would jump back, look at it, and jump forward again. I dared not look behind me, but I sensed them stopping and taking notes when they came to my easel.

I started hanging around the psych corner more often, but I had to make myself inconspicuous when graduate students were around. I heard the seminar had gotten off to a good start, with two or three very promising cases among the painting students.

The next Sunday I covered another thirty-six-by-twenty-inch canvas with casein. The finished product was a desert scene with a devilish-looking man jumping into a huge bowl of water beside a lone cactus and a single cloud in the sky. I put it out on my easel Tuesday just before the graduate students psychologically came in again one or two at a time. I twitched once, jumped back, jumped forward, and never looked back as they each stopped and took notes behind me.

In a few days, Kent and Dan told me that the seminar students had been talking quite a lot about a couple of really interesting cases, so I decided to prepare a painting for the third Tuesday. I conjured up a darkish, solid red woman with flaming hands, flaming feet, and chartreuse hair down her back. She was standing at the foot of some steps that led up to a city in the clouds.

By now, the psychs flocked straight to me and perched on the window sills behind me. I could hear them writing furiously and flipping the pages of their notebooks, but I never looked back at them, and I tried not to overdo the twitching.

On the fourth Sunday, I decided that I could not afford to spend much more time on this game because I was getting behind in my class work. I concluded that a calm landscape with clouds, sea, beach, and peaceful mountains would be an appropriate psychological farewell, but as I completed the serene scene, I couldn't resist putting some animated sunny-side-up fried eggs in the picture. Before I finished, I had painted more than twenty of them, marching by twos, hand-in-hand, from the mountain valley to the ocean. The lead pair of enormous eggs were stepping into the gentle waves.

The following Tuesday, the student analysts came in rapidly. I could sense about a half dozen of them fluttering behind me on the window sills. Suddenly I had an uncontrollable urge to see their faces as they seriously studied my marching eggs, so I got up to go get some brushes. I wasn't smiling, but I couldn't control whatever was playing out of my eyes. As I turned to walk in front of the psychs, I met the gaze of their leader and knew that he had instantly figured out my fraud—and that he knew that I knew that he knew. Without a word, all the graduate students suddenly leapt off the window sills in unison and stormed out.

For the next few days, I avoided the psych corner and my three best friends for fear of severe tongue-lashing. I soon learned this effort wasn't necessary since the whole psychology department was avoiding me—even Gardner, who usually didn't take psychology as religiously as the rest of them.

Finally Dan, normally a very controlled person, ran into me on campus and told me in heated terms that my little joke was the lowest thing he'd ever heard of in higher education.

"You are nothing but a hedonistic plebeian who has willingly violated the sacred trust of scholars merely to satisfy your dimwitted sense of demented humor!"

"Now, that's not fair, Dan," I said, trying to remain calm in my defense. "They did not ask our permission before they came sneaking in to study our personalities by observing our art. I saw no reason why I couldn't study their reactions to some unusual paintings without asking their permission."

He turned abruptly and left, choosing not to waste any more breath on such a degenerate, I guess. The silent treatment continued.

Two weeks later, Dan and I sat across the bus aisle from each other on the way to Birmingham to run in a track meet. After an hour of silence, I couldn't stand it any longer and said, "Dan, you're carrying this too far."

He slowly turned his disdainful gaze on me and replied, "You think you're so smart and that you've ruined the graduate seminar! Well, the graduate students told me that they're spending the rest of the semester in a very interesting study of what is wrong with you to make you do such a thing!"

The last I heard, they still hadn't figured out my problem.

20

Kent and Janie

NITA AND I WERE newlyweds during my sophomore year at LSU. She had been my high school sweetheart in Memphis and made a much better roommate than Ashlock and Mather back in the athletic dorm. We had a little garage apartment close to campus, so I was removed from most of the insanity of college dormitory life, though I continued to run track and took my meals at the athletic training table.

Kent, one of the three psychology majors who were my close friends, was about the only person in the whole sports program with whom I continued to associate much after I moved out of the dorm. He'd talk with me at the training table and often looked me up when I was studying at the secluded little spot I'd claimed in the remote stacks of the library. He was an unusual combination of tasteful brawn and super intellect. He had a tall, smoothly muscular body with blond hair and tan skin. His brain was full of facts about everything from proper chess moves to Shakespearean quotes to chemical equations. He'd had a taste of acting in high school and still sometimes seemed to enjoy an audience; he dabbled in writing and was occasionally published in the campus literary magazine; he loved great music. But his real passion was logic, and his normal conversational style was the intellectual argument.

A lot of people didn't like Kent because he was so blatantly smart and sometimes seemed aloof. Most of the athletes detested him, but he could pole vault thirteen and a half feet, so they had to tolerate him.

Among those who admired him, Kent got away with saying things that no one but the campus golden boy could have said. I was often amused with his analytical descriptions and prescriptions. He once told me, "Al, you bat your eyes too much. You have feminine eyes, anyway, so you really shouldn't be emphasizing them by batting them all the time." On another occasion, Kent was riding through Tiger Town with me when two extraordinarily beautiful girls crossed the street in front of us. Kent noticed I didn't avert my eyes from them and said I was reflecting some kind of psychological anxiety. He gave a full discourse on the kinds of weaknesses betrayed by looking too much at the opposite sex. "You're probably right," I told him. "Like the Bible says, 'The spirit is willing but the flesh is weak.'"

Most of the time we got along just fine, and I really appreciated his companionship on long bus trips to track meets when I needed someone who could converse about something besides girls.

Suddenly, in the late autumn of my sophomore year, his discussions with me turned to marriage and how to find the right mate. "How did you go about finding a wife?" he asked me one day at lunch.

"I just woke up married one morning." I laughed, but he didn't.

"You seem hesitant to talk about marriage. What makes you so evasive?"

"Why do you want to pursue it?" I asked, knowing I'd fallen into one of his analytical traps.

"You seem to have been quite fortunate in finding Nita. I've been looking for a wife for several years now, and I was just curious about how you handled the situation so successfully. I firmly believe that this is a matter for logic, not passion, and I want to be sure I have all the pertinent information available before I make a decision." His answer was matter-of-fact, and I was relieved this wouldn't have to be a long, drawn-out session.

I didn't altogether agree with his cool, logical approach to love and marriage—although I must admit he never exactly mentioned love—and I tried to laugh off his questions this time and every time afterwards when he brought up the subject.

And he did keep bringing the subject up. One day not long after the beginning of the spring semester, he got a little angry with me when I tried to laugh off another session of "How to Find the Right Mate." He said he was serious in his plans to get married, and he had just completed his study on the sociology, psychology, physiology, and just about every other-ology of the ideal wife. He knew her height and weight as well as the section of the country and size of town she would be from.

"The best possible wife would come from somewhere in Iowa, perhaps a town of about ten thousand," he said confidently. "Research shows that the most wholesome people in the world are reared there," he explained. "They grow up eating fresh farm-raised food; their environment is slow-paced and filled with enough silence to lessen the chances of anxiety syndromes; they're not poverty-stricken; they have good genes. So that's where I'm going to find my wife."

"Oh," I said, sucking in my cheeks. "How do you plan to do this?"

"Simple," he said. "The track team needs six to eight people for the Drake Relays in Des Moines this April. I only have to vault thirteen feet to qualify to go. I can do that easily. I'll ride up with the team, and if I need some extra time, I'll catch a bus back later."

"But, Kent, you just don't go off and find a wife in three days," I protested. "Everyone knows you're bright; no one argues with you. I know you're against being swept off your feet and falling into starry-eyed, unreliable love, but you just can't do this. It's not that simple!"

"It is and I will."

He made the team for the relays, but I didn't. He left with the group but didn't return with them. About four days after everyone else had gotten back, he appeared at my secret study place in the library, pulled up a stool, and said, "Well, I found her."

"You don't go find a wife in one week," I said.

"I found her," he persisted.

"So what happened?"

"We got there and I found out my event wasn't until the third day. So I caught a bus and rode up to the agrarian area out from Des Moines. I stopped in a couple of small towns and got the feeling that the research I'd read was absolutely right." He said he got back to Des Moines the day before his event and saw a caravan of cars drive up and park at the stadium parking lot. As the passengers got out and walked across the pavement, he saw a pleasant-looking girl who attracted him. Being the smoothie he was, he walked up to her, introduced himself, and told her he had a theory that Iowa girls make the best wives in the world. She evidently took the bait and told him everything he asked. She was a senior majoring in mathematics at a small Iowa college. She was the next to the oldest of five children and had spent her youth on a farm just outside Hancock, population 10,598. Her family had rented out their farm and moved into town during her high school years. Her father had injured his back in a tractor accident, and in town he could get a job that wasn't so physically taxing.

"She gave me the impression of having at least an average IQ," he said objectively, "and she seemed perfectly well-adjusted and happy. From what I could gather, she has had the proper exposure to agricultural experiences, silent places, education, good food, and exercise. In addition, I felt a certain attraction to her honest wholesomeness, and she was not unattractive. So the next day, I proposed to her and she accepted."

"Didn't she ask you any questions?"

"Not many. A lot of my assets are self-evident, and she probably would not be interested in those that aren't. Besides, the average woman is so flattered by a man's appreciation of her good qualities that she seldom requires any other recommendations. At any rate, I'm going back in June, and we'll be married in her home town."

"I guess you know what you're doing."

"It's really the only way to do it, Al. It's exactly the way I planned it."

For the rest of the semester, they communicated by letters and telephone, and he told me that with each communication the relationship was getting better and better. "I've sought out the best possible mate, and I know I am the best for her," he would say often.

I told him I was happy for him, but I just couldn't get used to this idea of marrying by formula.

"It's not a formula, Al; it's just intelligence," he insisted.

Summer passed with no word from Kent. Then one rainy day in early autumn, I looked up from my books in the library stacks, and there stood Kent with his dripping new bride.

"I want you to meet Janie," he said. I immediately stood and shook her wet but forthright hand. She was about five feet six inches tall with no really outstanding features. I remember thinking that she looked like an attractive girl who had been dipped in water. She was thin-framed and her oval face was decorated with an appropriate handful of freckles. She seemed very pleasant.

Kent said they'd found a small apartment, and he wanted us all to get together soon because he wanted Janie to meet Nita. When I told Nita, she suggested we invite them over first so they would have more time to get comfortable with their housekeeping. We did, and five days later they appeared promptly at six-thirty at our door. Janie, although no longer wet, looked as if she'd been rough-dried. Her mousey brown hair was combed in no particular style; it just sort of grew in various stages toward her neck and eyes. She was still charming, I thought, with an unpretentious, uncultivated beauty.

After supper, we sort of scooted over to the little area we called our living room. Early into our visit, Kent turned to Janie and said, "You need to sit straight; you shouldn't slouch like that."

"What do you mean?" Janie asked, submissive but obviously a little embarrassed.

"Ladies need to sit like this," he said, and he demonstrated, throwing back his shoulders and placing his knees together and feet side by side on the floor. "Look at Nita; she's sitting with her back straight, but you're slumped. I just don't want you to be bent out of shape by the time you're thirty-five."

Nita tried to change the subject, and Janie sat stiffly in her chair for a while. Eventually her loose limbs fell into a more casual arrangement as she got over her embarrassment and joined in the conversation. Fortunately, Kent was too wound up in some logical argument to chastise her again.

The next week, they invited us to their apartment for supper. As we were eating, Kent said, "Janie, your dress is crooked." She straightened it without seeming to lose her composure, such as it was. Shortly he criticized her again. "A little of your underskirt is showing, Janie. You really need to be more careful." He turned to Nita. "Janie has got to learn a few things about dress and cosmetics. These things were evidently not very important in her part of the country. Do you mind taking her with you the next time you shop and giving her some pointers on fashion and make-up? Janie, look at Nita there; she is so well harmonized. Her skirt and blouse are just perfect and her make-up is very becoming but not overdone."

Nita was too embarrassed even to try to change the subject, and Janie protested weakly, "Kent, it just doesn't work out that way with me. Mama always said you can't make a silk purse out of a sow's ear, and I just don't have what it takes to look like Nita."

"I think you should at least work at it; there are always methods to improve yourself," he said with something near disgust in his voice.

In the awkward pause that followed, I decided it would be a good time to start raving about Janie's raisin pie. I told her I always got hungry for raisin or mincemeat pie in the autumn, and hers was perfect. She brightened and told me her mother had taught her how to bake.

"Yes, we can tell," Kent said flatly. "Everything she bakes is very plain—nothing you can't get down on the farm. I was really hoping we could have served something a little more elegant for our first dinner guests."

The rest of us looked down at the remainder of the pie and the delicate lattice crust that Janie had so carefully woven over the dark, fragrant filling.

"Well, I thought it was a very elegant raisin pie, and it's one of my favorite desserts," I said cheerfully. A little while later, when we'd left the table and Nita and Janie were talking, I said to Kent, "Are you trying to completely reshape Janie? You wanted someone who came from that part of the country; they happen to love raisin pies up there."

"All of this is relative," Kent said knowingly. "Even though Iowa is the heart of America and the people there have wonderful qualities, they still need to grow and raise their level of sophistication. They can't just stay raisin pie-ish all through life."

I disagreed and told him he was going to ruin his perfect wife if he wasn't careful. We continued to have similar little arguments now and then, but they never seemed to endanger our friendship. And Janie continued to be her genuine pleasant self—as sweet as raisin pie could be. She was really quite attractive in her simplicity and in some ways even sharper than Kent. She had gotten a job in LSU's administrative offices just after they married and soon worked her way up to assistant to one of the vice presidents because of her efficient handling of statistics. But Kent wanted a classier wife.

Toward the end of November, we went with Janie and Kent to Tiger Stadium to see LSU play North Carolina, which was ranked number one in the nation. As we walked in, Kent said to Janie, "Remember to control yourself and don't act like the rest of these animals—no screaming and jumping, okay?"

"Is it all right if I scream and jump?" I asked.

"Oh, I don't care, Al. I think football is a ridiculous sport, and if you have to be rowdy to enjoy it, go ahead. I just came to please the rest of you."

Nita was naturally sedate at the game—she never makes a scene, being too shy to stand up and yell in front of people, even though they're not watching her—but Janie and I were continually leaping to our feet and cheering or booing, and Kent was continually pulling Janie back down and saying, "Look at Nita;

she's sitting calmly. You don't have to be like all these other people."

There were other times when Kent forced Janie to stay in her niche, I guess to emphasize his superior taste and intellect. Early one spring evening, Nita and I were walking down Main Street in Baton Rouge and happened to see Kent standing very properly outside a department store, waiting for Janie to get out of the movie across the street. He had gone to a different one that was already over. He said he allowed them only one movie a month because any more would be a waste of money on low entertainment. When he had suggested taking in some intellectual film for that month's ration, Janie had remarked that she wanted to see "Red River," with John Wayne.

He had insisted that she go alone to the movie of her choice even though she tried to convince him she would rather go with him. "She evidently needs some cheap escapism every so often, so I try not to deprive her," he explained, "but I don't intend to turn my mind to mush with her." Nita and I waited with him until Janie came out, asked her how it was, and went in for the second show after they left.

This indulgence of her unsophisticated taste was rare. He much more frequently tried to "improve" her. We all went swimming together about four months after the movie incident. Nita, who never learned how to swim, was content just to get wet and then sun bathe until she dried out, but Kent insisted on teaching her how to swim. He worked patiently with her in the water while Janie and I sat in the sand and talked. Occasionally, Kent would walk over for a few seconds to say, "Janie, straighten your back," or "Straighten your suit." Janie was wearing a plain black suit in the legitimate style of the day, but it looked about two sizes too big for her; she had the ability to make everything she wore shift to one side. She tried to adjust it but couldn't really do much to make it better. "Kent, I can't be what you want me to be," she said, and even in her exasperation she didn't whine but seemed to be apologizing.

"You can't sit out here in public with your bathing suit slopped around that way," he instructed. "You don't have to be a slouch just because you were reared on a farm. If you walk straight, sit straight, and dress straight, it will help you to think straight," he concluded as he turned to go try to teach Nita how to float.

Janie turned her honest face to me and asked, "Do you think I can ever please Kent? I don't seem to do anything right."

"You'll be fine," I said lamely.

"It's really getting to me," she said, and that was the first time I ever heard her complain.

When Kent finally gave up on teaching Nita to stay above water, we drove them home. Afterwards, I asked Nita how she would describe Janie.

"What do you want me to describe about her?" she asked.

"Well, is she pretty or ugly or plain or pitiful or what?"

"Oh, Janie is very attractive. She's just a little gawky."

"That's kind of what I thought. Do you think Kent is justified in his constant nagging of her?"

"Oh, no. He's only succeeding in making her worse. I predict she'll either leave him or become a total whimpering simp before this marriage goes very far," she said.

I agreed that Kent wasn't helping the situation, but I couldn't imagine this wholesome, all-American farm girl walking out on a marriage. Kent had said she attended church regularly in spite of his constant criticism of her church's doctrine, and I believe a commitment to one husband was strongly bound up in her tenacious faith. I just hoped Kent would eventually mature enough to appreciate her for what she was.

On several occasions, the four of us went dancing together, and this was one activity in which I outranked even Janie in clumsiness. Nita and Kent would do their Fred-and-Ginger routine on the dance floor while Janie and I sat at a table and talked about agrarian things. Occasionally we would venture out onto the dance floor and do the best we could, and at those times it seemed for some strange reason that we achieved an equilibrium within our clumsiness—a sort of controlled chaos. I remember that, as she danced in my arms, she was light and gentle, almost flowing—when I wasn't tromping on her toes. Kent would never dance with her. When we were all back at the table, Janie and I began to discuss the psychology of dancing, but for once Kent did not want to be intellectual. "It's just a graceful form of exercise," he said as he dragged Nita back out for another dance.

Kent finished his bachelor's degree in psychology and liberal arts at the end of summer with a 3.91 grade average. He must have goofed up somewhere. The day after graduation, we went over to say goodbye as they loaded up the car. They were moving to Georgia, where his family was, and he was going to work in some kind of scientific research. The last thing I heard him say before they rolled away was something about how poorly Janie had packed the boxes. We talked about them for a while, but time and absence make other people's problems grow less important.

I finished my bachelor's degree the next spring, and we moved to Memphis, where I taught art. I finished a master's at LSU during the summers, and about ten years after Kent and Janie had left Baton Rouge, I was awarded a teaching grant that allowed me to study for a year at the institution of my choice. I chose Stanford. In the late spring of my year there, I got a message to go to the Art Department's office for a phone call. It was Kent. To this day, I don't know how he traced me—maybe through LSU's alumni office. He told me that he and Janie and their two children were living in Marin County across the Golden Gate Bridge. He wanted us to come visit. We made plans for dinner the following evening at six.

I am usually punctual, but I had no idea how bad the traffic between Palo Alto and San Francisco was until we were in the middle of it. When we finally got across the Golden Gate, I almost never found their address. We arrived about an hour late. Their expensive, multilevel house was built into a bluff that overlooked a cove and, farther away, the bay and San Francisco twinkling in the fog. Kent greeted us; I apologized; he said it was all right. We went in, and Janie, who looked pretty much her sweet self, showed us their two boys, ages three and five. They were properly trained; Kent told them to go to bed, and we never heard a squeak from them again. We went on a brief tour of the house and were standing on a big deck enjoying the view of the bay when Janie said, "Let's hurry and eat so dinner won't get cold." We walked through the sunken living room and den and up several steps to the dining room that was lit only by candles flickering in the bay breeze.

We sat and talked politely about trivia as Janie brought out an elegant meal of steak and shrimp, some kind of savory rice, and a perfect spinach souffle, but Kent was embarrassed at the brand of wine she started to pour and ran next door to borrow a bottle of the kind he insisted he'd told her to get. When he got back and we finally began to eat, Nita commented on how romantic the setting was—the candles, the open window overlooking the bay, the soft music in the background, the olives in the rice. Kent, in his clinical voice, said, "This is probably the appropriate time to tell you, Al, that Janie has been hopelessly in love with you ever since I introduced you to her."

"Kent, that's unfair. That's a terrible thing for you to say!" Janie said in a pained but assertive voice.

"I have concluded that this is the appropriate time to do it," he said, commanding more authority.

"Well, you have always preferred Nita to me," Janie retorted.

"That's an entirely different subject," Kent said. "You have been through a complete analysis, and this thing you have for Al was the key to that analysis."

"I guess now you want me to say that I secretly hate Nita because you always wanted me to get my hair done like hers, dress like her, and sit up straight like her."

"If you wish."

Nita and I sat there, fumbling with our food and trying to pretend that we had not been hit with a boulder. I made some kind of meaningless comment; Nita was silent. Kent turned to me and said, "You know that I'm a practicing psychiatrist."

"No, I didn't know that."

"And Janie has had lots of problems since we left LSU. Two years ago, I finally convinced her to go through a total analysis, and I think she's getting better now. At least she's starting to admit some things about her psyche."

Janie brought out a fancy dessert. Nita tried to control the conversation by complimenting it and the rest of the meal, but there was not much hope of saving the evening. After dessert, we moved, appropriately, to the sunken living room, where Kent lectured about his collection of paintings. We all sat and talked stiffly, and after a while, Kent observed, "You notice that the conversation has not been the same since I told you I am a psychiatrist."

"When did you decide to go into psychiatry?" I asked, trying to keep us above the surface. "I thought you went to Georgia to do some kind of scientific research."

"I entered medical school not long after we got to Georgia. I stayed there for the extra two and a half years in psychiatry and then did my internship out here in San Quentin Prison. I'm now with one of the largest mental health clinics in San Francisco." He abruptly turned to look at Janie, who was just sitting there quietly. "Janie, get your hair out of your eyes." She automatically raked her fingers through her limp hair, and Nita, who had been sitting in shocked silence, tried to ask her about the children.

"Why did you come to San Francisco," I asked Kent.

"Because of the firm I'm with and most of all because I wanted to get as far away from Georgia and my family as I could. I don't allow Janie to go back to Iowa, either. Her family came here a few years ago and forced themselves in to visit, but they haven't come back. If Janie ever were to go back there, she'd just pick up more of her old bad habits."

We talked clumsily for a few more minutes, and I suggested to Nita that we'd better start back since it would take us at least two hours to get home. She readily agreed and we excused ourselves. Kent and Janie said they understood and walked us out to the car. Just as we got there, Nita discovered she had left her jacket in the house. Kent went back with her. While we were waiting, Janie looked away from me and said, "All those things Kent said about my analysis were absolutely true, Al." Before I could think of anything harmless to say, Kent had come back with Nita and asked us to come visit again. We said we would. We didn't.

Five years later, I tried to find out if Kent was still in San Francisco; he wasn't listed in the telephone directory or in the listing of practicing psychiatrists. We often wonder if Janie is still with him or if she wandered off somewhere with her own psyche. Wherever she is, I'm sure she sits with her dress crooked and her hair out of place.

21

Mama and Sonny Boy

AFTER FINISHING MY BACHELOR'S degree in art at LSU in the spring of 1950, I decided to take a graduate painting course there. Hoping to spend some time outside, I asked the course instructor, Louis Guglielmi, if some of my required paintings could be of landscapes and structures. He gave his permission, and I spent the first week of July roaming all over Baton Rouge.

I was driving my '39 Ford down Lakeshore Drive when I came across a visually intriguing house next door to the old Huey P. Long home. The design and construction were not unusual; it was a typical two-story colonial house—red brick with white columns and a coat of arms displayed over the door. The lawn was manicured and decorated with pink and white oleander, but the shutters were all closed and the house looked vacant. It drew me with an indescribable, almost haunting appeal.

I made a preliminary sketch and showed it to Guglielmi, who said, "It's just a house."

"But this house has a strange feeling about it," I insisted. He gave his permission for me to paint it.

The next day, I drove back to the house, which was situated between the Drive and the lake on the tip of a little peninsula. I parked in the shade across the Drive from the house and rigged up the back of my car as an easel. Traffic from the other homes went down one side of the peninsula or the other but seldom around the tip. I was able to work with very few distractions, forgetting the real world as I grew more and more absorbed in getting the mood of the house and landscape on canvas.

I painted every afternoon from one till four or five but never saw any trace of life around the house. After about a week, I decided the house was empty or the owners were on vacation. Then one afternoon, I noticed a long, green, old automobile creeping from behind the house and onto the Drive. As it passed me, I pretended to be preoccupied with my painting, but I noticed two people in the car. About ten minutes later, I sensed the car easing up behind me and parking on the other side of the Drive.

I saw a man of medium build, probably in his thirties, help a very wide elderly lady out of the car and across the Drive toward me. As she tottered across with her little bitty steps, I could see that she was about seventy-five years old, short, and weighed at least two hundred pounds. She wore lots of thick lipstick and makeup, and her hair was dyed Mercurochrome red.

Her escort squinted so much that his eyes were almost completely concealed. His sandy brown hair just stuck out of his head as if it had never been combed. He wore what we used to call a sun suit—casual pants with a pajama-looking top—and sandals with no socks.

I introduced myself as they stepped up and looked at my painting.

"How nice!" she exclaimed. "You're painting our house! Sonny Boy, look at that! Isn't that nice?"

"Sure is, Mama," her escort replied in a high-pitched, sing-songy voice.

"I think it's so nice that you're painting our house! Isn't that nice, Sonny Boy?"

"Sure is, Mama," he sang again.

"What do you plan to do with this painting, young man?" she asked me, her makeup cracking as she smiled.

"Well, I hope to get a good grade for it in my painting class at LSU."

"Oh, you're an art student! Do you think you might sell this painting?" she asked.

"I could," I answered nonchalantly.

"Well, you be sure and show it to me when it's finished," she said.

I told her I would, and they turned to walk slowly back to the long, green car, which then eased back to the house.

Two days later, I thought I saw someone playing peek-a-boo with me from behind the large shrubbery near the house. About five times, I saw a head jut out and pull back behind the oleander. I'd decided the haunting surroundings had induced my mind to play tricks when suddenly I saw Sonny Boy coming across the lawn, shuffling and skipping in a snaking route down the lane and across the Drive to my set-up.

"Mama sent you these," he said melodically as he held out a chicken salad sandwich on a paper plate and a cold bottle of Coke.

"Oh, thank you," I said, a little perplexed but very happy to see the refreshments since I was always hungry and thirsty at that age.

"*Don't* for-*get* to *show* the *pic*-ture to *MA-ma*," he sang, going up the scale and starting back down on the last syllable.

"I won't forget."

"Don't forget to show the picture to Mama," he repeated, same tune. He turned and zigzagged back to the house, hopping and circling around the shrubs and trees in the yard and stopping several times to peek back at me from behind them.

The next day, as I was getting close to finishing the painting, Sonny Boy started his peek-a-boo game again and eventually danced from shrub to tree to my easel.

"Mama sent you these." This time a saucer of cookies accompanied the Coke. Again I expressed my sincere appreciation, and again he sang his refrain: "Don't forget to show the picture to Mama."

"Oh, I'll show her."

"Don't forget to show the picture to Mama," he sang as he turned and did his peek-a-boo dance back to the house.

I was a little disturbed by this grown man in a sun suit who walked and talked like a character in a Shirley Temple movie, but I didn't let myself be driven from my spot. Two days later, I finished the painting and, heeding the numerous exhortations, drove back to show it to Mama the following Saturday morning.

I walked up to the mysterious door with my painting about eleven o'clock and rang the bell. After what seemed a long time, the door cracked and Mama's layered face peered out at me. She didn't remember me at first, but when I told her who I was, she asked me in, looked at the painting briefly, and exclaimed, "Oh, how pretty, how nice!" Then she took me by the arm and led me through the downstairs rooms on a sight-seeing tour. She showed me all the old paintings and family portraits, the silver-ware from Europe, the rare pieces of furniture. I thought this was all interesting and was receptive at first, but after about forty-five minutes, I began to get anxious to leave because I could tell she wasn't going to stop any time soon. I told her I needed to get back to campus.

"Oh, of course you do," she said apologetically, "but there are just one or two more things I think you'd like to see."

As she showed me some vases in the hallway, I got up my nerve to talk business. I finally managed, "Are you interested in my painting?"

"Well, yes. Would you sell it to me?"

"I think I could if you'd like to have it."

"How much do you want for it?"

"Oh, forty-five dollars," I wagered.

"Why, that's not bad at all! I'll go get a check."

While she was writing out the check, I realized that I hadn't shown the painting to Guglielmi for class credit yet. "You know, I haven't put a frame on it," I said. "I can put on a strip frame and bring it back Monday or Tuesday ready to hang. You keep your check until I bring the painting back."

"No, no, you take the check. I trust you," she said, handing it to me. I didn't even look at it as I stuck it in my pocket and made my getaway.

When I showed the painting to Guglielmi, he said it was pretty good. "You know, there is a sort of mysterious quality about the house. Is it really that mysterious?" he asked. I didn't know then just how mysterious it was.

Tuesday morning at eleven o'clock, I hauled the framed painting back to Mama's front door, where I again waited quite a while before the door cracked open. She took me in her parlor and had me lay it down on the floor so she could look at it. "That's very fine," she said; "I'm very happy with it."

I thanked her and turned to leave, making it almost to the door before I heard her call, "Young man, young man! Sonny Boy wants to see you."

"Me?"

She tottered to the foot of the spiral staircase, cupped her hand around her mouth, and called in a shaky soprano, "Cu-coo-oo, cu-coo-oo."

From way back up near the rafters I heard an echo "cu-coo-oo" and the shuffling of feet. Soon the shuffler appeared, leaning out of the dark from the bannister at the top of the stairs.

"The young man's here," Mama announced pleasantly.

"I'll be right down," Sonny Boy sang.

While I waited in curious bewilderment, Mama explained she was too heavy to go up and down the stairs anymore, so she was more or less confined to the first floor. "Sonny Boy's very good to come when I call."

I looked to the top of the stairs, and there came Sonny Boy dancing down the steps in his sandals and sun suit. His hair was wild and his eyes were still squinted almost closed. He shuffled up to me and sang, "Hello," in a little three-note song. Then he just stood and grinned at me like a very tall child.

"I bought the painting from the young man," Mama told him.

"Oh, how wonderful," he said. Then he directed his squinted eyes at me and announced, "I have something to show you. Follow me."

As I followed him down the hall that divided the bottom story in half, I started to feel abnormal because I wasn't dancing, too. We went out the back door and through another that opened to five connecting garages. We went through the first two garages, which housed the long green automobile and another old car. Then we entered the middle garage that was piled with junk and pieces of draped furniture barely lit by one weak globe in the ceiling. There were no windows and the only way out was through the other garages; the front entrance was barred.

Sonny Boy sidled over to a tall lump in the middle of the debris just under the light globe. Suddenly he yanked off the big canvas tarp that covered it to reveal a wooden Indian. Then he crouched beside it with his mouth open in a and his face fixed on mine as if he'd just shown me Christmas and was waiting for me to exclaim over it.

"Don't you think that's the most beautiful wooden Indian you've ever seen?" he prompted.

"Well, I haven't seen many wooden Indians, but that one surely is nice," I said politely.

"Mama let me buy it three years ago. *It* cost *lots* of *MON-ey,*" he said, making a strange song out of the second sentence. "I come out here to look at it almost every day. It's the most wonderful thing in the world!"

I was getting edgy by this time and kept repeating that I needed to leave. I opened the side door and made my way through the first two garages into the sunlight, with Sonny Boy shuffling along behind me. I started around the side of the house and had almost made it to the front yard when I heard Sonny Boy panting, "Young man, young man, let me show you something."

"What?" I said in three syllables, scaring myself with my melodious response.

"Looky up *they*-er," he sang up the scale, starting back down on the second syllable of "there." He was pointing up to a second-story window over which two big spotlights were mounted. "Every night people drive out here and park under the trees across the road," he continued. "I wait about thirty minutes; then I turn the lights on them." He laughed a little tune at himself.

I turned to go again and had gotten almost to my car when Mama called from the front porch, "Young man, come here a minute."

I went, wondering why I had such good manners.

"You didn't sign your painting," she told me.

I went back in and found to my dismay that I had indeed not signed it. "I'll bring my paints tomorrow and sign it for you," I said and finally got away.

The next morning, I returned at my usual time, eleven o'clock, rang the door bell, and waited for the door to crack open. When it did, Mama asked me in and told me Sonny Boy had already hung the painting upstairs in the music room. "It's the last room on the east side; Sonny Boy told me he hung the painting over the piano," she said.

I took my paints and brush and ventured up the spiral. When I reached the top and took a step into the hall, I saw an open door straight ahead of me. It was almost impossible not to look through the door into the room, where a very tall, very thin woman in a long, sheer, blue negligee stood by the foot of a large canopy bed. A few feet from her stood a round electric fan on a tall pedestal, which blew her very long black hair and negligee gently about her.

I looked quickly away and went on into the music room, a little embarrassed at disturbing the woman's unusual privacy. It took me about five minutes to mix my paint to the tone I needed and plant my name in the grass. Once while I worked, I glanced over my shoulder and saw her staring from the room at the end of the hall. She didn't look crazy. She didn't smile or frown. She just looked.

When I finished my work and walked into the hall, she was still staring and billowing in the breeze. I went downstairs and told Mama, "I sure appreciate your buying the painting." She smiled and waved at me as I drove away.

About a week later, I went to get a haircut at the Tiger Town Barber Shop on the LSU campus. While sitting in the barber's chair, I noticed a photograph of Mama's house on the front page of the *Morning Advocate* another customer was reading.

"What is that?" I blurted out, pointing to the photograph.

"Haven't you heard about the Bochman ordeal?" the barber asked as he snipped. "Old Mrs. Bochman has died and her relatives and children are stirring up a big stink about the will."

I borrowed the paper and read that eleven relatives had flocked from Georgia to contest Mrs. Bochman's will. She had died mysteriously a week earlier—the day after I last saw her. The will was read only a few days after her death, revealing that she'd left her entire estate, worth about fourteen million, to Herman Goodwin, who had been the Bochmans' nurse since he was about seventeen. Mr. Bochman had died mysteriously in his sleep five years earlier.

There was also a photograph of Goodwin, whom I recognized as Sonny Boy, his wild hair and squinted eyes unchanged. He was quoted as saying that no one but himself and Mrs. Bochman had been in the house during the entire month of July.

Another paper reported that the Bochman family believed Goodwin had been negligent in not giving their mother the medication she needed several times a day. There was also evidence that the will had been changed three months before her death, but the autopsy results showed no signs of foul play.

Sonny Boy's claim that no one had been in the house disturbed me. I had been there three times and had watched the house all month. And who knows how long the tall, thin lady had stood in front of the fan upstairs? I felt I should tell somebody Sonny Boy had not told the truth, but I had to report to Treadwell School in Memphis for a teaching job in less than two weeks. I wasn't even sure if my information was pertinent to the case.

I went to Miss Louise, LSU's fifty-year old maiden librarian and general source of all knowledge. I told her the whole story and asked her if I was supposed to do anything.

Even Miss Louise didn't know what I should do, but she did know a graduating law student and called him to arrange a meeting for me. I met the law student the next day and told him the story. He advised me not to get involved and risk missing my first day on the job in Memphis. "I'll follow the case and contact you if I think you are needed," he reassured me.

I figured I could trust a graduating law student to do the right thing, so I packed and embarked on my career, thinking I had done all I could do. For the next six months, I expected everyone I met to be an officer of the law coming to subpoena me. No one ever contacted me, and Sonny Boy and Mama finally faded into the past.

Four years later, I returned to LSU in the summer to take two courses required for my master's degree. The past came back, and on my second day there, I headed for the library. Miss Louise saw me walking toward her and smiled knowingly.

"You want to know what happened to Sonny Boy, don't you?" she asked and immediately began to fill me in. "Three months after Mrs. Bochman was buried, the relatives had the body exhumed and there were more hearings. About six months after you left, Sonny Boy was declared the sole recipient of the fourteen million dollar estate. He sold the mansion, built a ranch house outside of town, and married a lovely twenty-seven-year-old blonde."

"Have you seen him?" I asked.

"Yes."

"How does he look?"

"You wouldn't know him, Al," she said.

That evening Miss Louise joined me and a group of graduate students at a popular restaurant downtown. During our meal, she nudged me and pointed to a man getting up from a table not far from us. "That's Sonny Boy," she whispered.

His hair was combed and he had eyes. He wore a light-colored, summer-weight suit with a tie and appropriate shoes and socks. He walked in a normal gait out the door, got into a white convertible, and drove away, leaving several young women staring after him on the sidewalk.

22

Cry-at-will Elvie

REELFOOT LAKE IN FLAT northwest Tennessee is known for its rare and intriguing beauty. It was created during the great earthquake of 1811, when the land that is now its bed sank and the Mississippi River ran backwards to fill it up.

They say the lake gets its name from a club-footed Chickasaw Indian whose father, the chieftain, named him after the way he walked. Reelfoot fell in love with a beautiful, bright-eyed Choctaw maiden named Starlight, but the Chickasaws and the Choctaws were enemies, and Starlight's father wouldn't allow her to marry the limping suitor. Reelfoot went back home and languished until he decided he would just have to kidnap her. He gathered some braves and rode back to sweep her away. His father, who had also opposed the union, relented when he saw the lovely Starlight riding into their village and threw a big wedding party for the couple, but the conventional gods were angered at the whole affair and sank the earth beneath Reelfoot's marriage bed, covering the village with the backward-rolling Father of Waters. They say the moans of the lovers can be heard from the depths of the lake to this day.

Reelfoot's water is the color of thin, clear coffee, and it is continually silted by the troublesome soil of western Tennessee that dissolves like sugar when it gets wet. The siltation brings on more water lilies, smartweed, wild rice, mulefoot, rushes, and cypress and diminishes the perimeter of the lake. Its canals and bayous snake into the marshy land, hazardously dotted with cypress knees and stumps and the rotting remains of black walnut and maple.

This swampy lake, which seems out of place so far north, teems with game fowl and fish and is a haven for rare, beautiful, and sinister birds—great blue herons, American egrets, cormorants, anhingas, black-crowned night herons, bald eagles, swans, and black vultures that come at dusk to wait for young birds to fall from their nests.

Reelfoot is an unusual place, so it's appropriate that the most unusual student I've ever taught came from this area. Her name was Elvie, and she was a mysterious and beautiful creature. I first heard about her in the spring of 1960 when Mr. McDonough, a recruiting officer for Calgary College in Savannah, was describing her to the professors in the faculty lounge there. His job was to find underprivileged students deserving of financial aid to attend our small, very conservative liberal arts institution. Their presence lent a sort of poetic balance to the other half of the student population, which was made up of well-to-do, often overprotected and overindulged kids.

Mr. McDonough had just gotten back from a recruiting trip around Reelfoot Lake, where he'd found Elvie in a three-room swamp shack. She was to graduate that May from a small high school not far from Tiptonville. He emphasized that in all his years of recruiting he'd never seen a situation quite this odd: such an enigmatic and charming young lady out there in the stumps, living with a very poor and much older man and woman who, from what he could gather, were not even related to her. They had no money and not even anything to chink up the cracks in their floors and walls. He had never seen such destitution.

Elvie was just an average student, according to her high school principal, but she had expressed a desire to go to college. Mr. McDonough was impressed enough with her unexplainable qualities that he raked up some financial help, and she enrolled that fall.

Elvie's ephemeral presence on campus stirred up speculative conversation among students and faculty, but it wasn't until the spring of her sophomore year when I volunteered to chaperone a student social function that I saw for myself just what was inspiring so much talk. She gave a strikingly different visual impression. Her frame was very thin, but certainly not haggard. Her skin was pure white, almost too smooth against her very sophisticated black dress, and her long, black hair was always in place. But it was her eyes that did it. I expected to see big brown eyes in that face, but instead they were narrow cat eyes that glowed with a sort of unearthly, silverish fluorescence. They weren't quite beautiful eyes, but they were penetrating.

As I watched her that evening, she moved among the students in a strange way, always poised and collected and somewhat friendly, but always noticeably detached. She often listened in on the groups through which she wandered, but she seldom actually spoke.

After that night, I began to pay more attention to the rumors about her origin and the other comments that seemed to come from everyone. I heard she was considered one of the more attractive persons on campus and understandably so. It was said she had refused to join any of the sororities on campus, and this was an unheard of thing at Calgary. I heard she had no close friends and, although she always had dates for campus to-dos, no one ever asked her out more than once or twice. Once I got a call from an insurance salesman in town who was the local conqueror of females; he had seen a girl at an art exhibit and wanted to know who she was. After he described her, I told him she must be Elvie, but nobody really knew who she was.

She had perfect manners and speech and wore tasteful dresses, always in shades of brown and black. Anyone who just bumped into her would assume that she came from one of the older, richer families of West Tennessee. No one would have guessed she came from a shack by the lake.

One day in the faculty lounge, I overheard a professor discussing one of his students who seemed to cry all the time. He said he had asked an older student about the girl's problem and had been told, "Oh, everyone knows about Elvie; she can cry at a moment's notice. All you have to say is 'Cry, Elvie,' and she'll cry." The professor had begun to watch Elvie and the students around her before class, and he saw that almost every day someone asked her to cry, which she would do until class began—then she would immediately dry her eyes and appear undisturbed. It didn't seem to upset her. She was able to turn it on and off like a faucet. The professor said he had decided to stop worrying about her.

The next year, Elvie turned up in my beginning painting class, giving me a chance to observe her at close range in the friendly and informal atmosphere of the class. One day about four weeks into the semester, while I was having some general critiques with the students, one of the young men in the class asked me from across the room if I had ever seen Elvie cry. I was not at all comfortable with this public discussion of Elvie's problem, especially with her working at an easel not three feet away from me. I tried to change the subject, but the young man persisted and finally called out, "Elvie, the professor here has never seen you cry."

There was a long moment of tense silence as I agonized over how to get out of this situation. I certainly did not want to embarrass Elvie, and I had no desire to see her cry. I've never fully understood crying, and I usually get as far away as possible from anyone who is actively engaged in it. The student persisted, saying, "Elvie, why don't you cry for Mr. Allen?" That sort of peeved me, and I made it clear that it was not necessary for Elvie to cry for me.

I immediately felt a little guilty because I seldom show anger and I wasn't used to the result of it. The proverbial dread hush fell over the classroom, and I sensed everyone was disgusted with me for not being a good sport, though I wondered how I could have been a good sport by making someone weep. I decided to ask Elvie to help me smooth over the matter.

"Elvie," I said, "it will probably make everything better if you do cry. Can you really cry at will, Elvie?"

"Yes," she said, and she turned and looked at me as her eyes filled with tears that soon streamed down her face. We all looked at her, and I realized that she was really weeping and that she had been really weeping every day. Though it was amusing to the others, it didn't seem to be a game with her. I asked her to stop, so she took out a handkerchief and wiped her mysterious and sadly sparkling eyes.

After class, she and a couple of other students were lingering to clean up their brushes. I walked up to her and said, "Elvie, when you cry, you're really crying real tears, aren't you? This is not just a special ability you have; you cry because you need to cry, don't you?"

"Oh, yes," she answered softly, "I could cry anytime. I have been able to cry all my life at any time." She folded the old smock that had protected her coffee-colored sweater, smiled sweetly at me, and walked gracefully out of the room.

What was left of Elvie's last two years at Calgary passed rather rapidly. I often watched her from my office on the third and top floor of a grand old building erected in 1898. The rooms had sixteen-foot ceilings and high arched windows through which I could see the student union, the administration building, and just about anything that happened on campus. I watched her walking through the fall leaves, in the snow, and among the lacy greens and pinks of spring—always alone and always wearing brown or black. I had her in two more classes, but I never ever asked her to cry again. The students did, however. She was the campus weeper; if things got boring in the cafeteria or anywhere she happened to be, someone could always liven things up simply by saying, "Elvie, cry." I never heard of her not complying.

Although Elvie's standards of dress and grooming never fell below the impeccable, she did become noticeably thinner during her junior and senior years because, according to Mrs. Ruggles, the dean of women who kept close tabs on her destitute girls, she had opted to pay for only two meals a day in order to save money for art supplies. She did not complain or solicit pity; she just wept when given the opportunity.

By her senior year, everyone took the enigmatic presence of Elvie pretty much for granted, and on graduation day she received her diploma—in full tears, of course. She left Calgary armed with an elementary teaching certificate, a major in French, and minors in art and Spanish. Mrs. Ruggles continued to trace Elvie's progress in the world, and her information usually got back to the faculty lounge. We learned she did not go back to

Reelfoot after graduation but stayed in Savannah, where she had a summer job as a clerk in an art supply store. At summer's end, she headed west on a Greyhound bus with her savings of seventy-five dollars. Elvie had secured a teaching job in an elementary school at a little Arizona town near the Mexican border.

She got to Arizona two weeks before school was to start. Someone there told her she could see Mexico for very little money, so she got back on a bus and rode down beyond the border towns. In less than a week, all her money was gone. She was standing on a corner in Hermosillo, crying, when a Mexican businessman walked by and asked her what was wrong. When she told him she had no way to get back to Arizona to start her first real job, he offered her a two-day typing job in his office.

She made it back in time for the big pre-school social where all the new teachers were introduced to the school board members. She was still a little shaken from her Mexican detour and probably looked more pensive than usual as she stood by the wall with uninvited tears filling her unusual eyes. One of the school board members was evidently drawn to those eyes. He was a thirty-eight-year-old mining engineer, a confirmed bachelor who had been saving his money all his adult life. In two weeks they were married. The news spread at Calgary that Elvie had gotten a wealthy husband.

Elvie continued to teach for that first semester. Mrs. Ruggles reported Elvie's principal had written that she was one of the best first-year teachers he'd ever hired. She was wonderful with the children, who spoke mainly Spanish.

The following spring, I looked out my office window and saw two big cars roll up—a blue cadillac and a dark gray Lincoln. Elvie got out of the Lincoln. She looked pretty much the same except for maybe a few more needed pounds. She wore a dark gray suit. A tall, attractive, western-looking man got out of the Cadillac and put his hands on Elvie's shoulders for a few minutes. He had dark but handsomely graying hair and a kind face. Elvie kissed him and he got back in the Cadillac and left. Elvie turned, walked up the sixty steps to the Art Department at the top of the old building, and appeared in my doorway.

I greeted her and said, "I hear things have really gone well for you."

"Yes," she said. "It's been just wonderful." She told me that she and her husband had a big house in the middle of the desert with no one around for eight or nine miles. She had nothing but good things to say about the mining engineer, who was on his way to a meeting in Virginia. They had stopped in Memphis, where he'd bought her the new car. "I plan to go visit the folks out at Reelfoot and then head back to Arizona."

She seemed so happy and well established. I couldn't help but wonder if she still dissolved in tears. I didn't want to do anything to upset her, so I tried to talk about her teaching job for a while—but finally I had to ask, "Elvie, are you still crying as much as you used to?"

She looked straight at me and answered, "Oh, I still cry," and her tears started flowing over the rims of those strangely lit eyes and down her face onto her expensive suit.

"Are you going to cry forever?" I asked gently.

"I suppose so." She smiled through her tears, turned, and went down the stairs with several girls who wanted to see her new Lincoln.

23

Aunt Annie's Double Funeral

ONE LATE AUGUST DAY in 1964, Aunt Minnie's daughter Evalee called us in Savannah to say that Aunt Annie had died in her sleep and the funeral would be two days later at two o'clock at the Caruthersville Baptist Church. (No matter where their church memberships were, all good Allens were buried in Caruthersville.) So Nita and I left in plenty of time that Thursday morning to make the three-hour drive. On the way, I reminisced about the Bootheel and old stories about Aunt Annie that I'm sure Nita had heard many times before.

Aunt Annie was my favorite aunt, probably because she had raised my father—her baby brother—as her only child and doted on me as her only grandchild. She was a loving, hugging woman who dedicated her life first to God and then to cooking, canning, and cleaning. She was always humming or singing hymns. I especially remember how happy she seemed in the mornings as she hummed and kneaded biscuit dough, her two long, dark braids hanging down to her waist. After breakfast she would fasten her hair back into a neat bun. Once I asked her if she ever cut her hair, and she said not since she was fourteen.

Aunt Annie was the most religious of all the aunts and was a known Bible scholar and devotion leader. Whatever else she was, though, she was most famous for her reputation as a blood stopper.

It was common to see a field hand come up to the house in a half run, knock on the high porch floor, and ask for Miss Annie. When she'd come to the porch, he'd say, "Miss Annie! Miss Annie! Old Ned have cut his foot real bad with an ax!" She would calmly ask for the hurt man's full name; then she'd write it down and go by herself to the back bedroom. After a few minutes she'd come back out, lay her hand on the worried man's shoulder, and say, "He'll be all right now." He'd nod his head, say, "Thank you, ma'am," and walk back to work, confident that the crisis was over.

Sometimes an expensive car would drive up and a well-dressed man—maybe from another county—would get out to give Aunt Annie the name of a relative who had been hemorrhaging. In some mysterious way, she filled a big need in a county that had only one good doctor to call for accidents, illnesses, and giving babies.

A Baptist minister had given her the power to stop blood when she was about twelve years old back in Tennessee before her family moved to Missouri. He instructed her never to tell anyone else the secret of her gift until she was ready to give it up and pass it on to one or two males—the power always had to be transferred to the opposite sex. When she was ready to pass it on, she called me and John Barnes "Doolie" Thompson under the trees one Sunday afternoon and asked if we wanted the power. We were about twelve. I had always thought the whole thing was more than a little spooky, and I didn't really want anything to do with it. I didn't want to seem disrespectful, either, so I just sort of muttered, "I don't care." But Doolie told her he wanted it for sure, so she told us how she worked her magic. I was very uncomfortable hearing this stuff and don't remember any of the details; she did give us a verse from somewhere in the Old Testament to recite a certain way, but I put it all out of my mind.

Although she gave up her unique power, she continued to be known as the single one human in the Bootheel with the most complete Bible knowledge, and she made that knowledge evident every chance she got.

She was a mainstay in the Tyler Baptist Church until 1920. That was when they finished clearing the land and took up the railroad spur, and the town died. So Aunt Annie and Uncle Will moved to a place out from Cooter, where Uncle Will oversaw Mr. Thompson's big farm, and that's where they stayed.

Aunt Annie graced the Cooter Church for many years, but Uncle Will finally decided he was tired of hitching up the mules to drive in to town every week on his only day of rest. I guess this didn't bother Aunt Annie too much. She knew that "wherever two or more are gathered together, there the Lord is also," and she felt it was fully scriptural to conduct her own Sunday morning services in the living room. Several of her sisters and a few neighbors were usually there. If anyone else showed up during Aunt Annie's devotion, they were obliged to sit through it. She did almost all of the talking; Uncle Will just sat in the corner with an inscrutable smile on his face. During summers in the Bootheel, I often had my daddy pick me up and take me to Grandmother Bradie's on Saturday evening because Aunt Annie could expound on scripture so long that paid preachers who matched her would be fearing for their jobs.

Uncle Will tolerated all of this very well, but he didn't feel obligated to live his life by all of Aunt Annie's interpretations of the Holy Writ—at least not by her belief in total abstinence from strong drink. He never argued the point with her, and he certainly never got drunk. But the only time I ever saw Aunt Annie angry was the result of this conflict in philosophy.

It happened one year when Mr. Thompson talked Uncle Will into making some home brew. I was in on the secret and sworn to silence. I was too young to remember now exactly what it was they brewed or what they made it with, but I remember there was a lot of excitement and slipping around to the back shed behind the smokehouse, where Aunt Annie seldom ventured. One afternoon when she was visiting one of her sisters, Uncle Will along with Mr. Thompson and two strange men bottled the four large crocks full of the forbidden brew and hid it in the cool storage area under the house.

Several days later, while the members of the Women's Temperance League were gathered in Aunt Annie's living room, there was a sudden big bang. I was in the swing on the front porch when I heard it and naively went in to ask Aunt Annie what on earth it was. She was assuring me there was no imminent danger, and not looking quite as calm as she sounded, when all at once there were two more bangs, almost like a double blast from a shotgun. Soon it sounded as if someone were firing machine-gun rounds under the house. Aunt Annie told me to go on out and play, but I kept close by in the next room. Just about all four hundred bottles of home-brew blew up in an hour, and not one member of the Women's Temperance League was so impolite as to ask any embarrassing questions. They did leave a little early.

When the last of the teetotalers were gone, Aunt Annie flew into a rage such as I'd never seen, accusing Uncle Will and Mr. Thompson, who were both off somewhere, of once again secretly making home brew against her will and God's. When they did get back to the house, there were still a few bottles popping, and so was Aunt Annie. She met them on the porch crying, declaring that what they had done was wrong, evil, and against the law; that God was angry, and that her salvation was in jeopardy. Uncle Will just laughed, but she stayed mad for a week and didn't sing or even hum during that time.

When she did get over it, she was back to her old loving, happy self, secure in the knowledge that her soul and her house were spotless.

I never could figure her terrible fear of high winds and cyclones. She had such a strong faith in the power of the Lord and His promise of a blissful life after death that it was hard for me to understand why she was so afraid of dying in a cyclone. She often sang, "I'll fly away, oh glory," but I guess flying away must be different from blowing away. I know she had lived through many severe storms; she had seen the barn rebuilt three times during the thirty years they lived on Mr. Thompson's farm. Regardless of her belief in a home above the bright blue, she had a strong attachment to her storm house below the good earth.

It was a fine storm house, big enough for about sixteen people. Some late evenings when it was obvious a big storm was brewing, neighbors occasionally came by in time to take cover with us. There was something uniquely festive about laughing and visiting safely among the friendly canned goods in our lantern-lit hole while we could only imagine what havoc was being wreaked above our heads. But there were many times when Aunt Annie herded whoever was at home into the cellar to wait out a summer shower. "Lordy, it looks like it's gonna blow hard; let's go to the storm house, Alvin Junior," she'd shout, and we'd spend half the afternoon waiting for a little cloud to blow away. If the cloud came up during the night, I'd take a pallet and try to sleep on the dirt floor while she read from the Psalms or the Gospels, the most common passage being about the Master calming the tempest. Although she derived some comfort from the Word, she wanted the safety and security of her storm house whenever she was in doubt of the weather.

On our way through west Tennessee, I got so carried away telling Nita stories about Aunt Annie that I missed the Cottonwood Point Ferry across the Mississippi by about five minutes. We had to wait another forty for it to cross and come back. By the time we got to Caruthersville and found the church, we were a half hour late. There were still several people gathered outside, and a clump of relatives immediately came over to greet us—some I knew and some I had never seen before. Finally I saw Evalee and apologized for being late.

"It doesn't matter," she said. "We have a little problem about the service, and they're inside the pastor's office trying to work it out now."

The problem was that Aunt Annie had forgotten to move her letter from the Tyler Baptist Church to the Cooter Baptist Church when she and Uncle Will moved to Cooter over thirty years earlier. So the ministers of both churches were there to conduct the service, the Tyler minister claiming that she had personally requested that he preach her funeral the last time she saw him. "They'll have it worked out in a little while, I'm sure," Evalee said.

While waiting for the negotiations, I saw John Barnes "Doolie" Thompson (who was now the Pemiscot County

206 ❧ Al Allen

judge), his wife, and their three sons, who have since all grown up to be respected lawyers and businessmen in the Bootheel. After introductions and small talk, I took Doolie aside and asked if he remembered the day Aunt Annie gave us the power to stop blood.

"I've got the date written down in our family Bible," he said. Then he quoted the Bible verses and all the mumbo jumbo I had put out of my mind.

"That's amazing how you can remember all of that word for word after all these years," I said, impressed.

"Well, you've got to know it word for word or else it won't work. You are using it, aren't you, Alvin?"

"No."

"Well, it works," he said, and abruptly turned to talk to someone else, as if he were shaking the dust of his feet off on me.

Then some aunt whom I hadn't seen in twenty years came up to me and said accusingly, "You could come visit us sometime, but I guess a big-time professor doesn't have time for country folks."

She was gone before I could respond. Uncle Bob was nearby and told me, "Don't think anything about it. She thinks anyone with an education is a snob." Uncle Bob was really a cousin, Aunt Lou's son, but we called all older relatives aunt and uncle. He had been drunk for twenty-five years and always made good sense. The only times I had seen him act less than sensible were the two or three times I had seen him sober.

Finally Evalee appeared on the church steps and waved us all in. Nita and I, already sweaty and dusty from the long wait outside in the afternoon sun, squeezed into a crowded pew and tried to prepare ourselves for more discomfort. The building was packed, and no breeze came through the windows—just still, humid heat. We sat through an unusually long period of organ music; then the Cooter preacher, a very large man who had courageously kept on his suit coat while mopping his face and bald head with a white handkerchief, went to the pulpit and said, "Let us pray."

The congregation stood and he started in. I was teaching at a church college at the time and had endured a good many long prayers, but this man was eulogizing Aunt Annie and all the great Christians of all time. Fifteen minutes into the prayer, I felt Nita squeezing my arm and realized I had dozed off. I gripped the pew in front of us and managed to remain semi-conscious for the remaining five minutes of the prayer.

His "amen" brought little relief. As soon as he stepped aside, the Tyler preacher—a much smaller man—took his place and said, "Let us pray." From his first prayerful utterance, it was obvious that he intended to outdo the Cooter petitioner. We all stood for at *least* another twenty minutes, even though there were signs of restlessness and aching legs toward the end. By the time the second prayer was finished, the funeral had already lasted an hour.

Then a large woman (probably the wife of the Cooter preacher) got up and sang a very moving version of "The Unclouded Day" and another song that had at least six long verses plus a chorus repeated after each verse. When she sat down, a male quartet (most likely from Tyler) tried and failed to imitate Tennessee Ernie Ford's rendition of "Just a Closer Walk with Thee." When they finished singing, I heard distant thunder and noticed several people looking anxiously out and muttering about their car windows' being down.

There were no lights turned on in the building. It grew dramatically darker as the Cooter minister made a small talk, and I noticed the organist sneaking out the back. He ended his sermon by inviting those who wished to view the body to pass by. Not to be outdone, the Tyler preacher came up and repeated the invitation word for word.

The thunder was getting louder as people groped in the dark to get in line. There was no music for this morbid procession, just the respectful shuffling of feet on the squeaky, old wooden floor. In fact, everything was relatively smooth and quiet until Aunt Lou got to Aunt Annie's remains. All at once, she shrieked and leaped into the casket—all two hundred pounds of her—and commenced to implore in a shrill voice, "Don't go, Sister! Don't go!" I guess she didn't realize Aunt Annie had been gone for a couple of days already. Both preachers stood in a paralyzed state of discombobulation, and Nita started squeezing my arm nearly off. She had always been a little spooked by my people and by the whole flat, barren land of the Bootheel. I myself was not so much spooked as amazed at how Aunt Lou was able to haul her aged, bulky body into that casket and even more amazed that the whole pushrack didn't come crashing down. Of course, the casket wasn't very high; I suppose they make them higher now because of Aunt Lou.

After two or three minutes of shrieks, calm but drunk Uncle Bob went up and leaned over the casket. He spoke softly to his mother and with great effort, pulled her out. I couldn't help but think that in spite of her absolute disdain for the use of strong drink, Aunt Annie would have been grateful that one sensible drunkard was there to restore to her funeral some semblance of dignity. The rest of the crowd filed quickly by, but Nita and I refrained from viewing the disheveled shape Aunt Annie must have been in after Aunt Lou's visit.

It was dusky dark when we started slowly toward the cemetery on the outskirts of town. The procession was short a few cars after the extended service, and it seemed to speed up as the thunder and lightning in the southeast came closer. While we stood around the gravesite, the storm cloud got wicked and black and looked to be headed right at us. The dueling ministers were at it again, but even they had hurried up in the threatening weather. Suddenly there was a tremendous thunder clap, and the remaining mourners started running like mad for their cars. We were among them. From the shelter of our Ford, we could see them lowering Aunt Annie into the ground just as the storm hit and the wind blew leaves, limbs, and grass parallel to the ground. Three hired men started throwing in dirt triple fast, but one gave up and ran off. John Barnes Doolie Thompson was one of the last to leave. He didn't look up as he walked fast past our car in the downpour, and I knew he'd pass on the power to stop blood to one more worthy than I had been.

As the wind blew harder, we drove slowly away from the Bootheel, leaving Aunt Annie in her eternal storm house, where she would be forever safe from high winds, cyclones, and Aunt Lou.

New Brighton Area High School
New Brighton, Pennsylvania